Crohn's Disease

Titles in the Diseases & Disorders series include:

Crohn's Disease

Toney Allman

LUCENT BOOKS

A part of Gale, Cengage Learning

GALE
CENGAGE Learning

Detroit • New York • San Francisco • New Haven, Conn • Waterville, Maine • London

GALE
CENGAGE Learning·

LIBRARY OF CONGRESS CATALOGING-IN-PUBLICATION DATA

Allman, Toney.
  Crohn's disease / by Toney Allman.
    p. cm. -- (Diseases and disorders)
  Summary: "This series objectively and thoughtfully explores topics of medical importance. Books include sections on a description of the disease or disorder and how it affects the body, as well as diagnosis and treatment of the condition"-- Provided by publisher.
  Includes bibliographical references and index.
  ISBN 978-1-4205-0691-4 (hardback)
  1. Crohn's disease--Popular works. I. Title.
  RC862.E52A45 2011
  616.3'44--dc23
                                                    2011031203

Lucent Books
27500 Drake Rd.
Farmington Hills, MI 48331

ISBN-13: 978-1-4205-0691-4
ISBN-10: 1-4205-0691-9

Printed in the United States of America
3 4 5 6 7 15 14 13 12

Table of Contents

"The Most Difficult Puzzles Ever Devised"

Charles Best, one of the pioneers in the search for a cure for diabetes, once explained what it is about medical research that intrigued him so. "It's not just the gratification of knowing one is helping people," he confided, "although that probably is a more heroic and selfless motivation. Those feelings may enter in, but truly, what I find best is the feeling of going toe to toe with nature, of trying to solve the most difficult puzzles ever devised. The answers are there somewhere, those keys that will solve the puzzle and make the patient well. But how will those keys be found?"

Since the dawn of civilization, nothing has so puzzled people—and often frightened them, as well—as the onset of illness in a body or mind that had seemed healthy before. A seizure, the inability of a heart to pump, the sudden deterioration of muscle tone in a small child—being unable to reverse such conditions or even to understand why they occur was unspeakably frustrating to healers. Even before there were names for such conditions, even before they were understood at all, each was a reminder of how complex the human body was, and how vulnerable.

While our grappling with understanding diseases has been frustrating at times, it has also provided some of humankind's most heroic accomplishments. Alexander Fleming's accidental discovery in 1928 of a mold that could be turned into penicillin has resulted in the saving of untold millions of lives. The isolation of the enzyme insulin has reversed what was once a death sentence for anyone with diabetes. There have been great strides in combating conditions for which there is not yet a cure, too. Medicines can help AIDS patients live longer, diagnostic tools such as mammography and ultrasounds can help doctors find tumors while they are treatable, and laser surgery techniques have made the most intricate, minute operations routine.

This "toe-to-toe" competition with diseases and disorders is even more remarkable when seen in a historical continuum. An astonishing amount of progress has been made in a very short time. Just two hundred years ago, the existence of germs as a cause of some diseases was unknown. In fact, it was less than 150 years ago that a British surgeon named Joseph Lister had difficulty persuading his fellow doctors that washing their hands before delivering a baby might increase the chances of a healthy delivery (especially if they had just attended to a diseased patient)!

Each book in Lucent's Diseases and Disorders series explores a disease or disorder and the knowledge that has been accumulated (or discarded) by doctors through the years. Each book also examines the tools used for pinpointing a diagnosis, as well as the various means that are used to treat or cure a disease. Finally, new ideas are presented—techniques or medicines that may be on the horizon.

Frustration and disappointment are still part of medicine, for not every disease or condition can be cured or prevented. But the limitations of knowledge are being pushed outward constantly; the "most difficult puzzles ever devised" are finding challengers every day.

The Challenge of Crohn's Disease

When Jacksonville Jaguars quarterback David Garrard began experiencing stomach pains, he did not think it signaled a serious problem. Nevertheless, the team doctor sent him to see a gastroenterologist—a doctor specializing in diseases of the intestinal tract. Even when the gastroenterologist diagnosed him with Crohn's disease, Garrard was not worried. He explains, "I never heard of Crohn's so I thought, 'Whew, it's nothing.' I figured it couldn't be all that bad if I never heard of it. I'd take a pill and be done with it." As time went on, however, Garrard learned that living with Crohn's disease can be very difficult. He began experiencing common Crohn's symptoms such as cramps, diarrhea, nausea, vomiting, weakness, and weight loss. He went through treatment with different kinds of medications and changes in the foods he could eat, and finally, at age twenty-six, he had surgery to repair his intestines, which had been damaged by the disease. For a time, he could not play football, but Garrard did not despair. He says, "This disease is just a pain in the butt—literally. But you can't let setbacks beat you down because there are so many things in life that can do just that if you let them."[1]

Many people, like Garrard, have never heard of Crohn's disease, but that does not mean that it is not a serious illness. Living

An incurable inflammatory bowel disease that can damage the intestines over time, Crohn's disease causes diarrhea, painful gas, rectal bleeding, and an inability to eat normally.

1. Abdominal Pain

2. Diarrhea

3. Rectal Bleeding

4. Weight Loss

5. Arthritis

6. Skin Problems

7. Fever

8. Stunted or Delayed Growth in Children

9. Canker Sores Inside the Mouth

with the disease can be difficult, and fighting it can require courage. Crohn's is an incurable inflammatory bowel disease that over time can damage the intestines and cause often embarrassing symptoms, such as diarrhea, gas and pain, bleeding when going to the bathroom, and the inability to eat normally. People who suffer with Crohn's are often hesitant to talk about it. Garrard, however, is one person who is open about his Crohn's disease. He wants to raise public awareness about the consequences of the disease and to encourage others, especially children with Crohn's, to get the best treatment possible and to fight to live a normal life. He says:

> When I learned how many children suffer from Crohn's disease I decided I had to speak out more to raise awareness and prove to them we can fight this and win. . . . It is

a disease that talks about going to the restroom and all of these awful things coming out of your body. I can understand why a child would never want to talk about that. But someone needs to be a voice and help raise awareness for this and I realize that is my calling.[2]

Whether diagnosed as a child, a teen, or an adult, people living with Crohn's often have to face both emotional and medical battles. Though Crohn's is incurable, the disease is treatable, and new therapies and treatments allow most people to live normal lives. Like Garrard, many people with Crohn's hope for a cure while continuing to follow their dreams and achieve their goals. They do as Garrard advises: "Never give up."[3]

CHAPTER ONE

What Is Crohn's Disease?

On a website from Children's Hospital Boston of Harvard Medical School, a teen girl describes suddenly getting sick when she was thirteen years old. She lost a good deal of weight and was not growing normally. She suffered with frequent diarrhea every day, and she was extremely tired all the time. She says, "I remember thinking that the most mundane tasks were virtually impossible for me. Like how I was going to get to school, which was a couple of blocks away. How was I going to muster up the energy to walk there?"[4]

Another young woman, Annee, was twenty years old when she began to get sick, and she too was tired all the time and losing weight. She felt nauseated and had severe abdominal pain after every meal. She developed swelling and joint pain in one ankle. Next she developed painful canker sores inside her mouth and throat, rectal bleeding, and pain like arthritis in her knees. Once, she says, the pain in her knees was so bad that when she sat down on a curb, she could not stand up again.

Another sufferer, Alex, experienced joint pains, too, as well as bloody diarrhea, vomiting, fevers, and stomach pains. He, however, suffered these symptoms from the time he was a three-month-old baby. No one knew what was wrong with him for years. His mother remembers, "At age 5½ we went to see the doctors at Walter Reed Army Medical Center but by this time he weighed only 24 pounds and was almost 6 yrs old. I truly believed he would die."[5]

An Inflammatory Bowel Disease

All the symptoms that these individuals experienced occurred because they have one kind of inflammatory bowel disease (IBD) called Crohn's disease. An IBD is any disease that causes inflammation of the digestive or gastrointestinal (GI) tract. Inflammation is characterized by red, raw, and swollen tissues or organs and can occur anywhere in the body. When these conditions affect the intestinal tract, they can cause symptoms such as pain, fever, diarrhea, and bleeding.

One of the early symptoms of Crohn's disease is the development of canker sores inside the mouth.

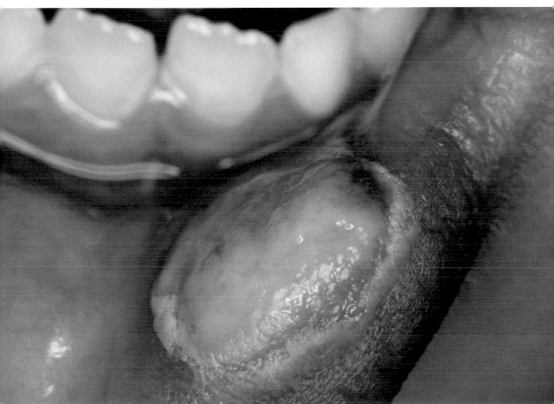

The two most common IBDs are ulcerative colitis and Crohn's disease. Both diseases are defined by where they occur in the GI tract and the damage that is caused in the affected parts. In order to understand these chronic, or long-lasting, diseases, it is necessary to understand how the digestive system works.

The Gastrointestinal Tract

Digestion is the complex process by which human bodies take in and process food for energy and growth and then eliminate the waste that is unusable by the body. The digestive tract is a series of organs connected by a long, winding tube that begins at the mouth. It is made up of muscles that push food through the system and break it down so that the body's cells can use its energy. The digestive tract is aided in this process by three other organs—the liver, the pancreas, and the gall bladder. These organs produce chemicals that help turn food into energy for the body. The digestive tract also includes cells that make enzymes and hormones that help break down the food. Enzymes are proteins that speed up chemical reactions, and hormones are chemicals made in one part of the body that control or signal reactions in other parts of the body.

Digestion starts at the mouth, where teeth and enzymes in saliva begin to break down food. From there, the food moves to the pharynx (or throat) and then to the esophagus, which carries the food to the stomach. When esophagus muscles push the food to the stomach, a ring-shaped muscle called the lower esophageal sphincter opens to let the food in and then closes to keep it in. The stomach is a very strong muscle that grinds and mixes foods while secreting acids and enzymes. Food in the stomach is turned into a pasty liquid called chyme.

Chyme is pushed from the stomach into the small intestine. The small intestine (sometimes called the small bowel) is a long, coiled, flexible tube made up of three segments. The first segment is the duodenum. Here food is broken down further with help from enzymes and chemicals from the pancreas and liver. The next segment is the jejunum. This middle section of the small intestine is lined with tiny finger-like projections called villi that allow nutrients in foods to be absorbed into the

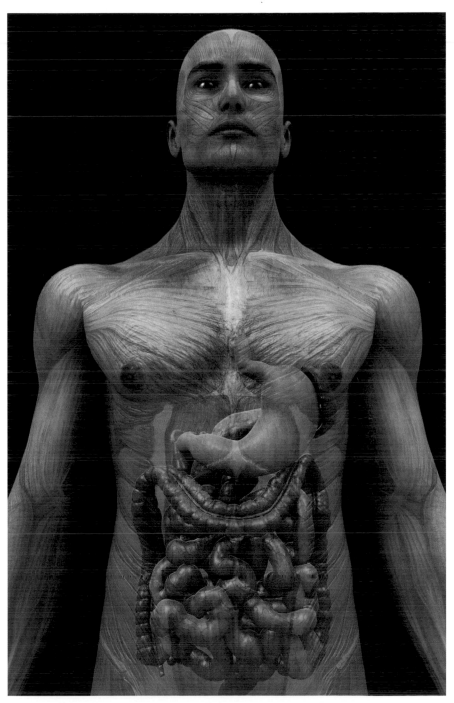

This illustration shows a view of the gastrointestinal system.

A Dangerous Complication

About 1 to 3 percent of people with Crohn's disease develop the complication called bowel perforation. A bowel perforation is a rupture or tear that can occur in either the large or small intestine. When it happens, air or intestinal contents escape from the rupture into the abdominal cavity. The symptoms may include abrupt and severe abdominal pain, nausea, fever, rapid heart rate, and low blood pressure. Perforated bowels require emergency surgery. The surgeon has to find the hole in the intestine and sew it up or remove the damaged part altogether and reconnect the intestine above and below the injury. He or she must also wash out the abdominal cavity if any intestinal matter has escaped the intestines. Bowel perforation is a life-threatening complication of Crohn's disease, but when promptly treated, most people recover without permanent damage.

A bowel perforation is a rupture or tear occurring in either the large or the small intestine, which may require emergency surgery.

bloodstream. The last portion of the small intestine is the ileum, which is the longest part of the small intestine. It is about 12 feet (3.7m) long in an average adult human body. As broken-down food passes through the ileum, more nutrients are absorbed into the bloodstream through the villi that line the ileum. It is only here, for example, that the vitamin B_{12} can be absorbed.

By the time the digested food has finished passing through the small intestine, all the nutrients have been extracted. Whatever is left over is the waste, which is pushed into the large intestine. The large intestine is also called the colon or the large bowel. It is a large, muscular tube, about 5 to 7 feet (1.5m to 2.1m) long. The waste, or stool, passes through the large intestine slowly so that any extra water can be absorbed by the body. By the time the stool reaches the end of the large intestine, it has become semisolid and easy for the body to push out. The semisolid waste is stored in the part of the large bowel called the sigmoid (S-shaped) colon until enough accumulates to be pushed into the rectum, where elimination begins. The rectum is like a receiving chamber that holds the waste, sends signals to the brain that elimination is required, and then uses its muscles to hold the waste until the person decides to go to the bathroom. Then the rectum empties the contents through the anus. The anus is the last part of the intestinal tract. It is made of muscles and is the opening through which waste is eliminated by the body.

Crohn's Disease and the GI Tract

Throughout the gastrointestinal tract, proper functioning is essential for digesting food and maintaining good health. When an individual has a form of IBD, something has gone wrong somewhere in the digestive tract. With ulcerative colitis, the inflammation always occurs in the rectum or colon (large intestine), but with Crohn's disease, it can occur anywhere along the GI tract, from the mouth to the anus. The inflammation is also not confined to one segment of the GI tract. Doctors Andrew S. Warner and Amy E. Barto of the Lahey Clinic of the Tufts University School of Medicine explain, "Crohn's disease may simultaneously involve different segments of the gastrointestinal tract where diseased segments of the intestine alternate with normal segments."[6]

Wherever it occurs, Crohn's causes that part of the GI tract to become swollen and develop deep sores called ulcers. The symptoms of this inflammation vary, depending on which part of the GI tract is involved. Currently, medical experts recognize five types of Crohn's disease. The most common type is called ileocolitis and affects the ileum and the first part of the colon. Symptoms of ileocolitis include weight loss, diarrhea, cramps, and pain in the middle or right lower part of the abdomen. Ileitis is the type of Crohn's that affects only the ileum, and the symptoms are the same as for ileocolitis. Gastroduodenal Crohn's disease inflames the stomach and duodenum. The symptoms are loss of appetite, weight loss, and nausea. Jejunoileitis affects patches of the jejunum, causing varying degrees of abdominal pain, diarrhea, and cramps after eating. Finally, Crohn's colitis affects the colon. Symptoms include diarrhea, rectal bleeding, and tears, ulcers, and infections in the anus.

Crohn's can cause a variety of symptoms in the people it affects. The diarrhea that almost always accompanies Crohn's disease happens because of the inflammation in the intestines. Inflamed cells secrete unusually large amounts of water and salt. The colon is unable to absorb all this extra fluid, so diarrhea occurs. The abdominal pain associated with Crohn's is caused by the inflammation and sores affecting GI tissues. Wherever they occur, they cause that area of the intestine to swell and thicken. This means that food cannot move normally through the intestinal tract, which causes pain. Bleeding may also occur, because the inflamed intestinal tissue breaks down, or because food scrapes against inflamed intestinal tissue and injures it. The inflamed portions of the intestine do not function normally, and this hinders the body's ability to digest and absorb food and nutrients properly. The inflammation can also cause significant discomfort or pain, and the more painful digestion becomes, the less likely an individual is to want to eat regular meals. Jennifer, who was diagnosed with Crohn's at age sixteen, explains, "Eating became a dreaded activity (because

Crohn's Disease

What is it?

It is a condition in which the walls of the digestive system—commonly the small intestine and colon—become inflamed, causing pain and possibly obstruction.

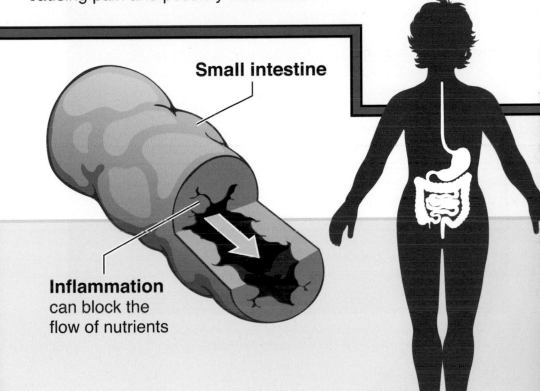

Small intestine

Inflammation can block the flow of nutrients

the pain seemed to increase after meals), and diarrhea a daily occurrence."[7] The combination of the body's failure to convert food to energy and a developed fear of eating can lead to weight loss.

Common Complications of Crohn's

All five types of Crohn's disease can lead to complications related to the ulcers and inflammation. Not everyone suffers from complications, and the effects of the disease can range

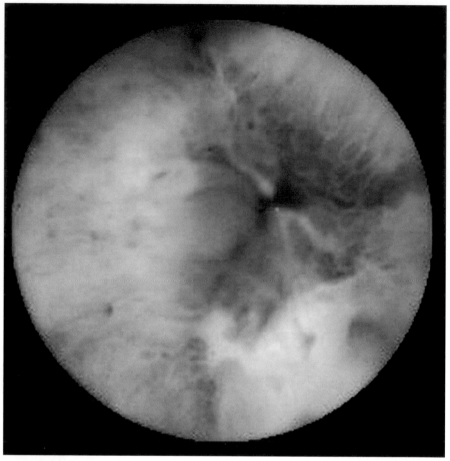

Inflammation in the lining of the ileum (the lowest section of the small intestine) has led to a stricture, or narrowing, of the intestinal passage.

from mild to severe. However, the majority of people with Crohn's disease experience one or more complications at some point in the course of their disease. When the disease first begins, the sores in affected segments of the intestine are small and shallow, but as time passes they become deeper. This process causes the intestinal segment to become scarred, stiff, and eventually narrower than normal. These narrow, localized areas are called strictures. If the intestine becomes very narrow, an obstruction can develop. Sometimes a piece of food, such as a piece of fruit or vegetable, gets stuck in the narrowed intestinal segment and blocks it. Other times, the intestinal segment narrows so much that it closes completely. At that point, food cannot pass through the intestine into the colon. It is trapped, and symptoms such as severe abdominal cramps, abdominal bloating, nausea, and vomiting appear. Obstruction is the most common complication of Crohn's disease. It is usually partial, and it causes increased pain, nausea, and bloating after eating. It usually affects the small intestine because this part of the intestinal tract is so much smaller in diameter than the large intestine, or colon.

Another complication occurs when ulcers become so deep that they eat through the intestinal wall. When this happens, a channel, or fistula, can sometimes form between the intestinal wall and another part of the body. According to the Centers for Disease Control and Prevention (CDC), about 25 percent of people with Crohn's disease develop fistulas, and in about 30 percent of them, the fistulas become infected. Internally, a fistula can be a connection between two adjacent loops of the intestine, which can interfere with proper digestion. It can also be between the intestine and another organ such as the bladder or vagina, and this can cause infections. More commonly, a fistula is external and makes a tunnel between, for example, the rectum and the skin, usually at the anus. In this case infection can cause burning, throbbing pain, and drainage or leaking from the anus. Often the fistula can result in recurring formations of abscesses.

Abscesses are the result of infections, and in the case of fistulas they are caused by the leakage of bacteria and other matter from the breach of the intestinal wall. An abscess is commonly called a boil. It is an accumulation of pus that the body has walled off in order to prevent an infection from spreading. Pus is made of live and dead bacteria and live and dead white blood cells that were part of the immune system's effort to kill the invading bacteria. In Crohn's disease, abscesses most often occur at the rectum and anus and they can be painful, not only when going to the bathroom but also when sitting and walking. Sometimes abscesses break and drain on their own, but other times, a doctor has to puncture and drain them. Abscesses that drain by themselves into the body can, in turn, cause new fistulas to form, such as between the rectum and the skin around the anus.

Serious but Rare Complications

Occasionally, the deep ulcers and fistulas of Crohn's disease result in fecal matter or intestinal bacteria leaking into the bloodstream. Then the infection can be carried throughout the body and cause an overwhelming infection called sepsis. Sepsis is a potentially life-threatening condition that causes high fever, chills, a rapid heart rate, and low blood pressure. If untreated, low blood pressure can damage body organs, such as the kidneys, liver, and lungs. Jennifer was hospitalized with this complication and remembers, "My experience with sepsis was one of the scariest side effects associated with my Crohn's disease."[8] Jennifer's sepsis was the result of a rare complication of Crohn's—a perforation, or rupture, of her intestine that allowed air to escape from the bowel and enter the abdominal cavity. This condition almost always requires emergency surgery to correct the rupture.

Most people with Crohn's do not experience life-threatening complications, but as a chronic disease, Crohn's can increase the risk for other serious diseases, including arthritis, eye inflammation, osteoporosis, and cancer of the small intestine or colon. No one knows why this risk occurs, but researchers believe that the intestinal inflammation process may trigger inflammation in other parts of the body in some people. Arthritis is a disease of the joints, such as knees, fingers, elbows, and shoulders. It causes inflammation, pain, swelling, and stiffness in the affected joints. Inflammation of the eyes can cause pain or blurred vision, but it affects only about 5 percent of people with Crohn's. Osteoporosis is a disease that causes weak, brittle bones. It can be a complication of Crohn's in older people who have had Crohn's for years. It can be a result of nutritional deficiencies, and as people with IBDs get older, it is estimated that osteoporosis may eventually affect close to 50 percent of them. The risk of cancer depends on how long the person has

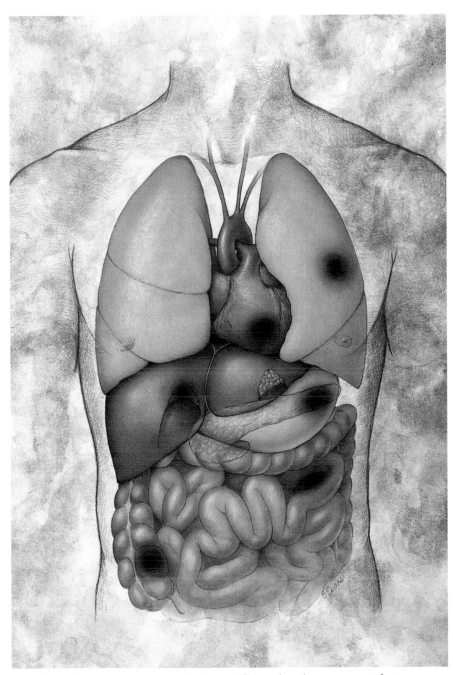

These dark spots are areas that are inflamed with sepsis, an infection that causes high fever, chills, a rapid heart rate, and low blood pressure.

had Crohn's and how severely the intestines are affected. People who have suffered with Crohn's for many years and perhaps have inflammation throughout the entire colon may have an increased risk, but the risk is small. The Mayo Clinic's website explains, "Despite this increased risk, more than 90 percent of people with inflammatory bowel disease never develop cancer."[9]

As adults age, they may face complications that younger people do not, but children and teens with Crohn's disease can have an increased risk of different kinds of complications. The disease can stunt their growth, delay puberty, and weaken bones. All these problems occur because young people are still growing. Failure to grow normally is a danger in about 15 to 40 percent of children with Crohn's.

Remissions and Flare-Ups

The majority of people with Crohn's disease do not suffer dangerous complications, but they do have to live with a disease that sometimes causes no symptoms and other times causes pain, side effects, and sickness. This means that Crohn's is not a constant disease. Usually, the disease follows a pattern of remissions and then flare-ups or relapses. Remissions—periods of time when the person has no symptoms—are longer and more frequent than periods of flare-ups, which are marked by acute symptoms. Flare-ups are unpredictable and vary with each individual. Some people have a mild form of Crohn's disease; others have severe Crohn's that frequently interferes with normal life. Doctors David B. Sachar and Aaron E. Walfish explain, "Crohn's disease almost always flares up at irregular intervals throughout a person's life. Flare-ups can be mild or severe, brief or prolonged. Severe flare-ups can lead to intense pain, dehydration, and blood loss. Why the symptoms come and go and what triggers new flare-ups or determines their severity is not known."[10]

Who Gets Crohn's?

Much is still unknown about Crohn's disease, but medical researchers have learned that Crohn's seems to be more common in the developed countries of the world. No research has been able to determine positively why this is the case, but researchers do know that Crohn's disease is more common among people of European origin than in other ethnic groups. It is three to eight times more common in Jewish people, especially Ashkenazi Jews, than in other Europeans. The CDC reports also that all IBDs seem to occur more frequently in urban areas than in rural areas and to affect more people in northern areas of the world than southern ones. In developed Asian countries such as Japan and Singapore, as well as in Hong Kong, the incidence of Crohn's has increased and approaches that of Europe and North America. In the United States African Americans are almost as likely as people of European origin to develop Crohn's disease.

No one is sure how many people worldwide are affected by Crohn's disease. The CDC estimates an incidence of between 0.1 to 16 people per 100,000 people around the world. This means that in the U.S. population, for example, about 1.4 million people have Crohn's. In all of Europe about 2.2 million people have Crohn's. In addition, in the United States and Canada, approximately 10,000 to 47,000 new cases are diagnosed each year. Crohn's disease also seems to run in families. Of the newly diagnosed cases every year, about 30 percent have another close family member who has an IBD.

Crohn's can affect an individual at any stage in his or her life, but the disease seems to develop most often in people who are relatively young. Although anyone of any age can get Crohn's, the usual age of onset is between fifteen and twenty-five years, but between 15 and 30 percent of cases are in children before the age of puberty. About 5 percent of people with Crohn's develop the disease before they are five years old. On the other hand, about 25 percent of new cases are diagnosed in people older than sixty. Why Crohn's develops at different ages in different people is not known by scientists, but there is some evidence that the extent of inflammation of the intestine is less in older people than in younger people. In 2007 researcher Hugh J. Freeman did a study that showed that elderly people who develop Crohn's more often have the type that affects the colon

Sick with Crohn's

On a website from the Department of Psychiatry at Children's Hospital Boston, a young teen reports her experience with Crohn's disease and its associated symptoms. She says:

When I first got really sick, it was my freshman year in high school. I felt like my stomach hurt but I went to school anyway. When I came home after school I threw up all day. I'd never been that sick—it was so bad. I had that for about a day and then all of a sudden I was fine. But then for the next month or so I was still getting stomachaches. For a while we thought, "Oh, it must be that virus I'm getting over." I was playing lacrosse at the time, so I was really busy. But the stomachaches got worse and worse. I was at a point where I was trying to eat and ended up bending over the table with really bad cramps. So that was my experience with cramps and loss of appetite. For me it was a big deal because I love to eat, but all of a sudden I just want some mashed potatoes and bread and nothing else.

"When I First Got Sick." Early Stages, IBD Experience Journal, Children's Hospital Boston, 2005. www.experiencejournal.com/ibd/child_earlystages.shtml.

(Crohn's colitis) rather than other portions of the intestinal tract. When children and teens develop Crohn's, they also may be more likely to develop Crohn's colitis than the ileitis that is more common in young adults.

A Mysterious Disease

Crohn's is such a variable disease—striking people at different ages, leading to different symptoms, and affecting different locations of the intestinal tract—that medical researchers sometimes wonder if they are dealing with different causes for the varying types. Theories about the cause of Crohn's disease have so far been unconfirmed by medical experts, but today researchers are working intensively to change that.

CHAPTER TWO

The Cause of Crohn's Disease

When television journalist Cynthia McFadden was eighteen years old, she was diagnosed with Crohn's disease. She felt burdened by guilt over the diagnosis because her doctor told her the disease was her fault. She remembers, "The gastroenterologist treating me told me I was responsible for my condition. That being a 'Type A' personality caused my illness." McFadden believed this incorrect assumption until she consulted another doctor, who explained that her Crohn's was not caused by her stress levels or because of her personality. She says now, "It took several years for me to believe I wasn't at fault. . . . I don't want anyone else to experience the psychological torment I felt thinking I was responsible for my condition."[11]

Though some in the medical community, like McFadden's first doctor, initially believed that Crohn's was brought on by an individual's actions, researchers now agree that this has no relation to the development of the disease. Warner and Barto explain, "It's not from something you ate or didn't eat, it's not from drinking too much alcohol or coffee consumption, it's not from stress, it's not from working too hard, and it's not from lack of sleep. We simply do not know what causes an IBD [inflammatory bowel disease]."[12] When Crohn's disease was first described in 1932 by American doctor Burrill B. Crohn, he speculated that

News anchor Cynthia McFadden was eighteen when she was diagnosed with Crohn's disease. It took a second medical opinion and several years of emotional struggle before she realized that having Crohn's was not her fault.

the underlying cause might be an infection. Today scientists believe that Crohn's has multiple causes and is related to the complex interaction of genetic factors, problems with the individual's immune system, and environmental triggers.

Crohn's Is an Autoimmune Disease

Crohn's disease is now generally acknowledged to be an autoimmune disorder, in which the immune system attacks body cells as if they were foreign invaders. The immune system is the complex network of defenses that the body uses to protect itself from disease and harm. A variety of immune system cells

Burrill B. Crohn

Along with two colleagues, Burrill B. Crohn was the first doctor to describe Crohn's disease. Crohn, born in 1884 in New York City, was the son of Jewish immigrant parents who valued education. At age thirteen the bright boy entered City College of New York, where he first became interested in science and medicine. At age eighteen he entered medical school at Columbia University, graduating in 1907. He became a respected physician, specializing in diseases of the gastrointestinal tract at Mount Sinai Hospital.

In 1932, after observing fourteen patients with common symptoms, he and his colleagues submitted a paper to a medical journal describing the disorder that they named "regional ileitis." (They did not know then that the disease could affect any part of the intestinal tract.) Almost immediately, other doctors around the world recognized the disease in their own patients. Crohn successfully treated many patients with surgery to remove damaged parts of the intestine, but despite his attempts, he could not discover the disease's cause. He searched for the bacteria he believed were responsible but was unsuccessful.

Crohn practiced medicine into his nineties. He died at the age of ninety-nine in 1983, best remembered for the disease named in his honor.

recognize, mark, and then attack any foreign invaders, such as bacteria or viruses, that might cause disease. For example, the inner lining of the intestine—the mucosa—contains many kinds of immune cells. Cells called macrophages are the sentinels. They recognize invaders and react by engulfing and eating the foreign substances. They then send chemical signals to other immune system defenders indicating that help is needed. Macrophages also release other chemicals that increase the flow of blood to the affected area, send pain signals to the brain, and cause swelling and inflammation at the site of the infection.

Other cells, white blood cells called B cells, respond to the macrophages' signals by producing antibodies. The function of antibodies is to bind to and chemically tag invaders so that they can then be targeted by immune cells. The proteins on the surface of any substance that cause antibodies to form are called antigens. Antigens are recognized as foreign and provoke an immune response. Antibodies latch onto the antigens of a particular foreign substance and mark it for destruction by other immune cells such as those called killer T cells. In the intestinal tract all these immune system cells ensure that dangerous outside substances cannot escape into the body and cause damage. They are destroyed before they can be digested and absorbed through the small intestine into the bloodstream. As long as the foreign substances are a threat, the immune system produces antibodies to fight them. Once the foreign substances are eliminated, the immune system turns off until another invader is detected.

Usually, the immune system attacks only foreign substances that threaten the body. The immune cells distinguish between cells that are "self" and those that are "nonself." Scientists call this tolerance of self. It means that immune system defenders such as B cells and T cells tolerate, or do not attack, body cells. Whenever B cells and T cells are made for an immune system response, they are chemically tested by the body for tolerance of self, to ensure that they will attack only foreign substances and not body cells. The whole immune system is programmed to ensure tolerance of self and to weed out and destroy cells that are not self-tolerant. Biology professor and immune system expert Lauren Sompayrac explains, "This strategy works very well, but occasionally 'mistakes are made' and instead of defending us against foreign invaders, the weapons of our immune system are turned back on us. Autoimmune disease results when a breakdown in the mechanisms meant to preserve tolerance of self is severe enough to cause a pathological condition [a disease]."[13] When an autoimmune disease is present, the immune system reacts to normal body cells as if their proteins are foreign antigens and produces antibodies against them.

The Autoimmune Process in Crohn's Disease

Though scientists are still not certain why autoimmune diseases develop, they are beginning to understand what is happening when the immune system goes awry. In Crohn's disease the immune system attacks the cells of the lining of the gastrointestinal (GI) tract, which produce mucus to protect the intestine from stomach acids and harmful bacteria and viruses. The tissues of the intestinal tract become raw and inflamed. The chronic inflammation in the GI tract is caused by immune system cells such as macrophages, B cells, and T cells attacking body tissues and cells as if they are foreign substances. Blood flow is increased; chemicals are released that cause swelling and send pain signals to the brain; intestinal cells are destroyed; protective mucus is lost. All the symptoms of Crohn's, such as poor digestion, pain, and diarrhea, are the result.

How the autoimmune process begins has yet to be discovered, but scientists do have theories about what triggers it. Microbiologists James Byrne and Thomas Tu explain:

> For Crohn's, as with most autoimmune diseases the immune cells that start attacking the body don't just slip past the [body's] testing system to act maliciously; they are somehow inappropriately activated into self-destruction mode. In the case of Crohn's disease, there seems to be no one [thing] that sets it off, rather it is expected to be a combination of environmental factors alongside a level of genetic susceptibility.[14]

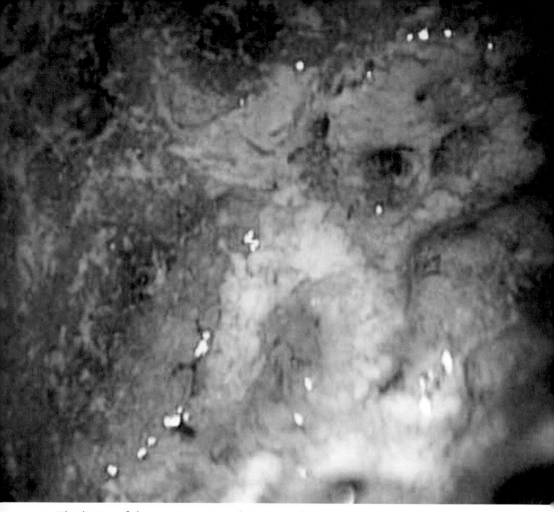

The lining of the gastrointestinal tract produces mucus to protect the intestine from stomach acids, bacteria, and viruses. In Crohn's disease the immune system attacks the lining, causing it to become raw and inflamed.

Crohn's Disease and Genes

Genetic susceptibility is an inherited increase in the risk of developing a disease. Usually, it is caused by variations or changes in a gene or genes that do not cause a disease by themselves but do predispose the person to develop a disorder under certain conditions. Genes are the packages of deoxyribonucleic acid (DNA) that control for how every living thing grows, develops, and functions. In humans genes are grouped together in bundles of twenty-three pairs of chromosomes, half inherited from the mother and half from the father. The way these genes combine produces a unique individual. The genes' coding instructions often determine each individual's abilities or disabilities and to which diseases a person may be more or less vulnerable. Most genes are the same for everyone, but variations in genes cause people to be born with different eye color, for example, or to have different blood types. Variations in genes are common and normal—everyone has them. Sometimes, however, these variations can increase the risk of autoimmune disorders such as Crohn's disease.

According to the National Institutes of Health, about 20 percent of Crohn's cases run in families because of inherited gene variations. If one parent has Crohn's, for instance, the risk that a child will also develop Crohn's is between 4 and 9 percent, thirty times more than the risk if neither parent has the disease. If both parents have Crohn's, the risk increases to 36 percent. In identical twins the risk is between 44 and 58 percent that if one twin develops Crohn's, the other will, too. However, even for identical twins—who share identical genetic makeup—genes do not account for 100 percent of the risk. So researchers know that a variation in a single gene does not cause Crohn's disease. Instead, researchers theorize that several genetic variations are involved in a predisposition to the disorder, which is then triggered in vulnerable people by something in the environment.

Today researchers have identified seventy-one genetic variants that are associated with an increased risk of having Crohn's disease. Some are linked to other autoimmune disorders such as asthma, diabetes, and rheumatoid arthritis, as well as to Crohn's. Most of the genes that have been identified are known to be involved with determining how the immune system works.

Genetic Variants That Increase Risk

In 2001 researchers at the University of Chicago and the University of Michigan discovered the first Crohn's gene. It is called NOD2, and it seems to code for, or direct, how immune system cells, particularly macrophages, recognize and detect bacterial invaders. An abnormal variation of this gene is shortened—about

3 percent of it is missing. The result is macrophages that are less efficient at recognizing the antigens of dangerous bacteria. Gabriel Nuñez, one of the research leaders, explains, "We found that the truncated [shortened] version of Nod2 is much less responsive to the presence of these bacterial components."[15] People who have inherited one copy of this variant have triple the risk of developing Crohn's compared to those who have a normal version of NOD2. People who inherit two variant copies, one from each parent, are about 40 times more likely to develop Crohn's. No one knows why a slow, inefficient response to bacteria would lead to the inflammation of Crohn's disease. Some scientists speculate that the defective response of macrophages perhaps causes other immune system cells, such as B cells and T cells, to have an exaggerated, prolonged response to the invader, causing inflammation in the intestine. Other scientists speculate that the variant gene causes an immune response to the normal, beneficial bacteria that live in the intestine, leading to a prolonged inflammation in the area. However, only about 15 percent of people with Crohn's disease have a shortened NOD2 gene, so it is only part of the answer to the cause of Crohn's.

After the NOD2 gene variations were discovered, researchers quickly found many more variations in other genes that seem to increase the risk of Crohn's disease. For example, in 2006 scientists identified a variation in a gene called CCR6 that causes immune system white blood cells to be overactive in the intestine, which can cause inflammation. In 2009 Alexandra-Chloé Villani of McGill University in Canada led a team that discovered another gene variant that increases the risk of Crohn's. The gene, called NLRP3, controls production of a protein that is the immune system's sensor for bacterial invaders. Villani theorizes that the protein is defective in people with an NLRP3 variation. Because the sensor is defective, she hypothesizes that the immune system response to an invader is weak, slow, or ineffective. She can see how this situation could lead to inflammation and the symptoms of Crohn's disease. Villani explains:

> When the digestive immune system's counter-attack is insufficient to clear the threat, there is a bacterial infiltration

in the intestinal wall through the first line of defence mechanisms. The digestive immune system will again try to repel the threat, but the effort may not be sufficient, and this usually leads to a vicious cycle that results in chronic inflammation in the intestinal wall. And that is Crohn's disease.[16]

A macrophage engulfs a bacterium as part of an immune system response. In Crohn's disease, macrophages become less effective at recognizing the antigens of dangerous bacteria.

Other research studies have identified areas of chromosomes where more genetic variants seem to increase the risk of Crohn's, but scientists have not yet identified the specific genes involved or how they control the immune system. The National Institutes of Health's National Center for Biotechnology Information explains that Crohn's disease is a complex trait, meaning that multiple genes at multiple locations contribute to the disease, but none of them cause the disease by themselves. In addition, scientists believe that different combinations of gene variations may cause different forms of Crohn's, with some variations triggering ileitis and others causing Crohn's colitis. Some combinations may cause Crohn's to develop in young children, while others lead to Crohn's in adulthood. Still, Warner and Barto say of all these gene variations, "They are only part of the story."[17]

Environmental Triggers of Autoimmunity

Most scientists believe that an environmental trigger starts the inflammatory process in genetically susceptible people. Jean-Paul Achkar, a physician writing for the American College of Gastroenterology, explains:

> In IBD it appears that there is an initial trigger such as an infection or something taken in from the diet or the surrounding [environment] that activates the immune system. However, the difference in those who develop IBD is that the immune system does not turn off once this initial trigger is eliminated. This leads to uncontrolled inflammation and attack on normal intestinal cells.[18]

One environmental factor that is known to increase the risk of Crohn's disease, says Achkar, is cigarette smoking. Smokers are more likely to get the disease than nonsmokers, but scientists do not know how smoking affects the immune system and the intestinal tract. Other medical researchers theorize that Crohn's can be triggered by an infection, perhaps a bacterium or a virus. Researchers suggest that in some cases an initial infection can trigger an immune response, but once the invader is successfully conquered, the defective immune system does

Western Diets

Because Crohn's disease is much more common in developed Western countries than in other parts of the world, researchers have speculated that diet may play a role in its development. These researchers have suggested that a diet high in fats, sugars, and processed foods is responsible for Crohn's disease. Support for this idea comes from the fact that people in developing countries, who eat a diet high in fiber and low in fat and meats, tend not to develop Crohn's disease. In one study, the diets of people who were diagnosed with an inflammatory bowel disease were compared to a group of people without the disease. The researchers reported that people with inflammatory bowel diseases ate more red meat and cheese before they were diagnosed than did the other group. In a laboratory study, researchers found that certain plant fibers could prevent intestinal bacteria from the GI tract from triggering an overactive immune system response. However, most researchers say that the connection between diet and Crohn's disease is doubtful. Other researchers find no connection between diet and Crohn's disease in their studies. A change of diet may ease the symptoms of the disease, they argue, but this does not indicate that Crohn's has a dietary cause.

One research study found that, preceding their diagnosis, people with inflammatory bowel diseases ate more cheese and red meat than any other group.

not turn off. Instead, it continues to react and causes a continual, out-of-control inflammation that leads to Crohn's.

One type of bacteria that researchers suspect may trigger Crohn's is *Escherichia coli* (E. coli). Many harmless kinds of E. coli live in the intestinal tract, but some strains can cause diarrheal infections. People can be infected by these bacteria if

Some researchers suspect that the bacterium *Escherichia coli* is a trigger for Crohn's disease.

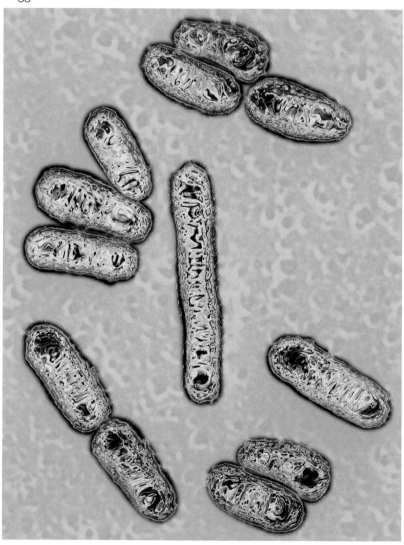

they drink water or eat food that has been contaminated by fecal matter from other infected individuals. New York professor of medicine Jill P. Buyon says that many people with Crohn's disease often show evidence of having been infected with E. coli. She also explains that certain cells in the intestines may have a molecular makeup that is similar to the molecular makeup of E. coli bacteria, and this similarity could confuse the immune system in genetically vulnerable people. This is called molecular mimicry, and it may be a trigger for Crohn's disease. Buyon says, "Molecular mimicry could ... play a role. There may be similarities between the structure of part of the E. coli bacteria and part of the colon cells. In lab experiments anticolon antibodies, found in the blood of people with Crohn's and ulcerative colitis, react against colon cells *and* E. coli."[19] The lab tests suggest that the immune system antibodies do not distinguish between the colon cells and the bacteria. Both are treated as invaders by the immune system.

Could Crohn's Be an Infection?

Some researchers argue that bacteria do more than trigger Crohn's—they cause it. The bacterium responsible, according to these scientists, is named *Mycobacterium avium* subspecies *paratuberculosis* (MAP). Despite its name, this bacterium is not the one that causes tuberculosis, but it is from the same bacterial family. MAP mainly affects cattle and causes an infection called Johne's disease. Like Crohn's, Johne's disease causes chronic inflammation of the intestinal tract. Cattle can harbor the bacteria without showing symptoms, but even if they are not obviously sick, infected cows shed the bacteria in their milk and into the environment. One of the main proponents of the theory that MAP causes Crohn's disease is John Hermon-Taylor, a Crohn's specialist and medical doctor at the University of London's St. Georges Hospital Medical School in the United Kingdom. Since the 1990s he has been researching MAP and its relationship to Crohn's disease. He concludes that MAP infections cause Crohn's in genetically susceptible people when they drink milk contaminated with MAP, which is not killed by the heat of pasteurization. About 68 percent of the cattle in the United States are infected with MAP, and Hermon-Taylor believes that the numbers are equally high in Europe and Canada.

Hermon-Taylor says that MAP infections are difficult to detect in humans, but it can be done by testing for the bacterium's DNA in infected people. He says:

> Human populations are widely exposed. . . . When validated methodologies have been used, most people with CD [Crohn's disease] have been found to be infected with MAP. In simple words, most people with chronic inflammation of the intestine (of the CD type) are infected with a mycobacterium which is a proven specific cause of chronic inflammation of the intestine. There are no data which demonstrate that MAP are harmless to humans. The overwhelming balance of probability and public health risk favours the conclusion that MAP are also pathogenic [disease-causing] for people.[20]

In Britain, Hermon-Taylor claims, 90 percent of people with Crohn's are infected with MAP.

Some scientists agree with Hermon-Taylor, but his conclusions are controversial. Most experts say that the theory cannot be supported by today's scientific evidence. Some researchers report that they have not found MAP to be present in people with Crohn's disease in their studies. Others do not agree that MAP has been proved to cause inflammation in people and argue that MAP is not the cause of Crohn's, but a result. They suggest that as a common bacterium, it simply infects or colonizes the intestinal tract of a person whose defective immune system cannot fight it. In addition, some studies of treating Crohn's with anti-MAP antibiotics have suggested an improvement of the inflammation, but others have not. In an article in the journal *Practical Gastroenterology*, L. Campbell Levy and Kim L. Isaacs wonder if MAP bacteria are "simply along for the ride" and conclude that "the MAP theory of causation in Crohn's disease remains neither definitively proved nor refuted."[21]

A cow is screened for *Mycobacterium avium* subspecies *paratuberculosis* (MAP). Some researchers suspect that MAP, which causes Johne's disease in cattle, also may cause Crohn's disease in people. The symptoms of both diseases are similar.

Many Possibilities

Another theory about the environmental cause of Crohn's disease is called the hygiene hypothesis. It suggests that the incidence of Crohn's and other autoimmune diseases in developed countries is a result of living in an environment that is too clean and sterile. According to this theory, people are not exposed to enough bacteria and germs in infancy, so their immune systems do not "learn" to react appropriately. As a result, their immune systems may overreact or fail to turn off when they are exposed to foreign invaders. Also, some theorists suggest, the normal bacteria that live in the intestinal tract are lost in too-clean environments, so the intestinal tract is out of balance and cannot fight off invading bacteria. Other environmental risk factors for IBDs that have been considered by scientists include growing up in urban areas, lack of sun exposure, food additives, some drugs and medicines, and even lack of breast-feeding for infants.

Canadian researchers Natalie A. Molodecky and Gilaad G. Kaplan have reviewed the evidence for all the theories about the environmental cause of IBD and conclude, "Despite years of investigation, the environmental risk factors that have been identified have not explained the pathogenesis [development or origin] of IBD."[22] When it comes to the cause of Crohn's disease, researchers still have more questions than answers.

CHAPTER THREE

Diagnosis and Treatment of Crohn's Disease

Diagnosis and treatment is often a lengthy and complicated process for those with Crohn's disease. Sometimes people suffer symptoms for years before they are correctly diagnosed. Accurate diagnosis is critical to the effective treatment of Crohn's, but its symptoms are similar to the symptoms of many other disorders. In addition, no single test is sufficient for diagnosis. Once patients are diagnosed, treatment may not be straightforward, either. Effective treatment may be a problem, explains the Mayo Clinic website, because "Crohn's disease affects each person differently, and people respond to treatments differently as well."[23]

What Is Wrong?

When symptoms first appear, Crohn's disease may be misdiagnosed as another intestinal disorder. A Canadian teen named Megan, for example, began suffering with abdominal pain and diarrhea when she was sixteen years old. Her family doctor was not sure what was wrong and tried to help her by recommending changes in her diet and getting her to reduce her stress levels. Then, after about two years, Megan went to see a gastroenterologist (a specialist in diseases of the gastrointestinal, or GI, tract), who diagnosed her with irritable bowel syndrome

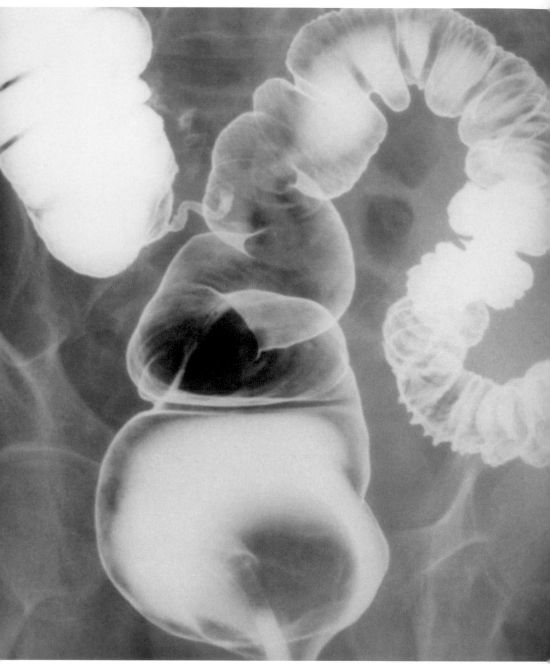

Shown here is a colored X-ray of the normal sigmoid colon and rectum (lower center) of a patient with irritable bowel syndrome (IBS). IBS symptoms resemble those of Crohn's disease.

(IBS). This disorder is very different from an IBD. IBS does not cause inflammation or any damage to the intestinal tract. It causes cramping, gas, diarrhea, and constipation because the intestine is not functioning correctly, but it is considered a syndrome, not a disease. Although apparently normal, the colon muscle contracts or spasms easily, perhaps due to stress or diet, in people with IBS. IBS is much more common than IBD, but it is not a serious disorder.

Megan's gastroenterologist changed her diet and gave her a drug meant to calm the colon muscle. As the months went by, however, her symptoms got worse instead of improving. Finally, the doctor performed several specialized tests that revealed four ulcers in her small intestine, and the doctor diagnosed her with Crohn's disease. After three years of symptoms, Megan had the diagnosis that made effective treatment possible.

Diagnostic Testing

One of the important tests performed by Megan's gastroenterologist was an endoscopy—a visual examination of the inside of the body with an instrument called an endoscope. This is a flexible tube with a tiny camera attached on one end. The camera is connected to an eyepiece or a television monitor so that the doctor can see any changes in a portion of the body. The tube is threaded into the portion of the intestinal tract that the doctor wants to inspect. One form of the procedure is called a colonoscopy; a colonoscope is threaded through the anus into the colon. During a colonoscopy, the doctor can also remove a tiny tissue sample for examination in the laboratory. The forceps used to get the sample are passed through a thin channel of the colonoscope. Under the microscope, the sample can be used to distinguish between Crohn's and, for instance, colitis caused by infection.

Most people suspected of having Crohn's also undergo a gastroscopy, or upper endoscopy, to examine the upper part of the gastrointestinal tract. In this procedure the endoscope is threaded through the mouth while the patient is sedated so that the doctor can see and get a tissue sample of the esophagus, stomach, and duodenum. This was the test that revealed the ulcers in Megan's small intestine. The test can also reveal inflammation and strictures. However, an upper endoscopy does not allow a doctor to see the entire small intestine, and since any part of the GI tract can be involved in Crohn's disease, specialized X-ray tests usually are necessary to examine the entire small intestine for damage.

An upper GI series is a set of X-rays taken after the patient drinks a chalky, white substance called a barium solution. The barium solution coats the esophagus, stomach, and small intestine so that they are outlined on the X-rays. This test detects inflammation, strictures, and fistulas. It can reveal how much of the intestinal tract is affected by Crohn's disease. Computed tomography (CT) scans are computer-aided X-ray techniques that provide more detailed images of the intestine than X-rays alone. They may be used to find abscesses and fistulas that do not show up with regular X-rays. Magnetic resonance imaging tests may be used to identify abscesses in the abdomen as well as to assess the ducts of the pancreas and the bile ducts that may be obstructed in Crohn's disease. At the Mayo Clinic, researchers have developed a specialized test called multiphase CT enterography (MCTE) that can find the source of any bleeding and identify abscesses and fistulas that have developed between loops of the intestines. The Mayo Clinic explains, "MCTE can image the entire thickness of the bowel wall, all of the long loops in the small intestine, and surrounding tissue."[24]

Additional Diagnostic Tools

All these examinations reveal inflammation, abscesses, ulcers, or fistulas, and they can help the doctor rule out other intestinal diseases and disorders such as celiac disease, lactose intolerance, gall bladder disease, or stomach ulcers. However, they are not enough for a diagnosis of Crohn's disease. Laboratory tests such as blood tests and stool tests are required to be sure that the symptoms are not caused by an infection or a cancer. Then, when the diagnosis of Crohn's seems accurate, the doctor uses lab tests to determine any other problems that might be caused by the Crohn's. For example, doctors look for signs

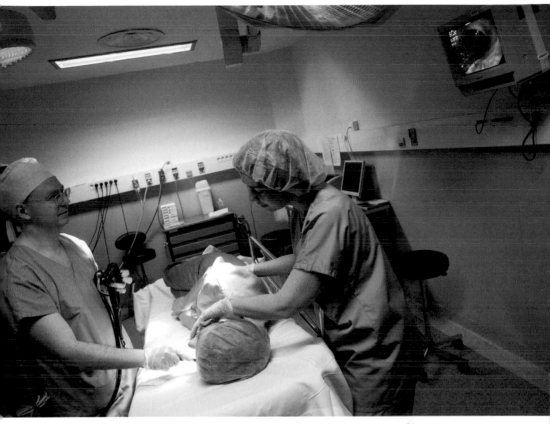

A gastroenterologist examines a patient by inserting a fiber-optic endoscope, or lighted tube, through the mouth into the digestive tract. The patient's digestive tract appears on the monitor (upper right).

of anemia (low level of red blood cells) from low iron absorption, malnutrition, or infections caused by fistulas that have allowed intestinal bacteria to escape into the body. They try to determine exactly which parts of the intestinal tract are affected and how severe the disease is. Only when the location and severity of the inflammation is known can the doctor begin to develop a treatment plan.

Crohn's disease cannot be cured, but today people have many treatment options, from medications to reduce inflammation and control the overactive immune system, to lifestyle

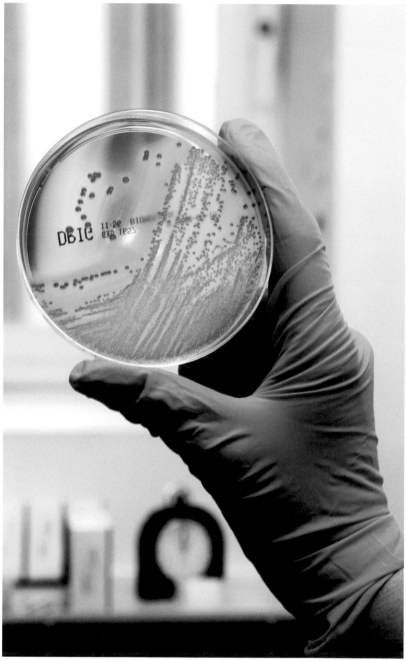

Laboratory tests of a stool sample are an important diagnostic tool in ascertaining that the symptoms of Crohn's disease are not caused by an infection or by cancer.

changes, to surgical interventions that repair damaged portions of the intestinal tract or remove obstructions. "The goal of medical treatment is to reduce the inflammation that triggers your signs and symptoms," explains the Mayo Clinic. "Doctors use several categories of drugs that control inflammation in different ways."[25]

Anti-Inflammatory Medication

Anti-inflammatory drugs are usually the first medications tried with Crohn's disease. One of the most common is called sulfasalazine. It is a pill, taken two to four times daily, that combines

When a Cure Is Not a Cure

Physician Arthur Schoenstadt, in an online article for eMedTV, has a warning for people with Crohn's disease. Many so-called natural cures for Crohn's are touted on the Internet or in other places. However, none of the claims for miracle cures with special diets, herbs, supplements, or other alternative treatments have been scientifically proved. Testimonials from individuals who have tried these treatments are not evidence. The people who tried them without success are simply not quoted. None of these treatments have been regulated or approved by the Food and Drug Administration. None have been studied with controlled research experiments. This means, according to the Mayo Clinic staff, that "manufacturers can claim that their therapies are safe and effective but don't need to prove it. In some cases that means you'll end up paying for products that don't work. . . . What's more, even natural herbs and supplements can have side effects and cause dangerous interactions." Schoenstadt agrees. He also says that the "natural" products can interact with prescribed medications. People should always be cautious and inform their doctors if they want to try alternative treatments.

Mayo Clinic Staff. "Alternative Medicine: Crohn's Disease." Mayo Clinic, August 8, 2009. www.mayoclinic.com/health/crohns-disease/DS00104/DSECTION=alternative-medicine.

an aspirin-like medicine with a sulfa antibiotic. It works in the colon to quiet inflammation and reduce pain. Although it works for people with Crohn's colitis, it is not as helpful for people with other kinds of Crohn's disease because the drug needs the benign bacteria in the colon to work. People who are allergic to sulfa drugs cannot take this medication, and in some people it can cause side effects such as headaches, nausea, and indigestion.

Today newer drugs with the aspirin-like compound but that are sulfa free have been developed. They are called aminosalicylates, or 5-ASAs, and there are several kinds. These medications reduce inflammation in the colon and the small intestine. This class of medications usually works well for people with mild to moderate Crohn's. The medicines can treat acute symptoms, help people stay in remission, and prevent flare-ups. Although aminosalicylates can cause side effects, the Crohn's & Colitis Foundation of America (CCFA) says, "Up to 90 percent of people who cannot tolerate sulfasalazine are able to take other 5-ASAs."[26]

Corticosteroids

Sometimes a person's symptoms are acute, severe, and very painful, or the individual finds that aminosalicylates are not effective enough or cannot treat the area of the intestinal tract that is inflamed. When that happens, people may use drugs called corticosteroids to fight inflammation. One common corticosteroid is called prednisone. Corticosteroids are powerful anti-inflammatory drugs that can treat and quickly stop painful flare-ups. They suppress the immune system at the same time that they reduce inflammation. However, only 70 to 80 percent of patients respond to corticosteroid treatment, and corticosteroids such as prednisone cannot be used long-term. They may cause a remission of Crohn's disease, but they are safe only for limited treatment periods and they can cause dangerous side effects. Corticosteroid use can make people more likely to catch infections because their immune systems are suppressed. People also can suffer with edema (retaining fluid in the body), high blood pressure, acne, weight gain, diabetes, mood swings, insomnia, and osteoporosis.

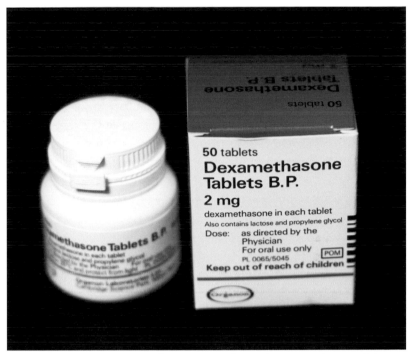

Corticosteroids are anti-inflammatory drugs that treat the painful flare-ups of Crohn's disease by suppressing the immune system and reducing inflammation.

Jennifer, for example, was given prednisone by her doctor when her Crohn's disease was diagnosed. It worked immediately to relieve her inflammation, and she used it off and on frequently to fight the painful flare-ups that kept occurring. She describes her condition after a year on prednisone:

> Unfortunately, despite the reprieve the medication provided me from my symptoms, I fell victim to its nasty side effects. . . . I had gained a substantial amount of weight as well as what some physicians and patients often refer to as moon cheeks—a rounding of the cheeks. . . . I also experienced moderate mood swings that came on with absolutely no warning. . . . I came to despise the drug.[27]

Because of problems like Jennifer's, doctors prescribe corticosteroids at the lowest dose possible for the shortest amount

Vitamin D and Crohn's Disease

In 2010 physician John White and a research team from McGill University in Canada reported that their laboratory studies suggest that vitamin D can treat or prevent Crohn's disease. The researchers were studying cancer cells in their lab and discovered that adding vitamin D activated two genes that are sometimes deficient in people with Crohn's. The genes are NOD2 and beta-defensin 2. Both are involved in regulating immune system functions. They are particularly important for determining how macrophages recognize and attack invaders. According to White, vitamin D appears to enable these genes to correctly direct the body in fighting intestinal infections.

White explains that people who live in northern countries are often deficient in vitamin D because it is absorbed from sunshine, and northern places have less sunshine than southern areas, especially in the winter. He recommends that people at risk for Crohn's, such as family members of those already diagnosed, should take vitamin D supplements to reduce the risk of developing Crohn's. He also believes that further research may show that the vitamin is a good treatment for people already diagnosed with Crohn's disease.

Research at a Canadian laboratory suggests that vitamin D can treat or prevent Crohn's disease.

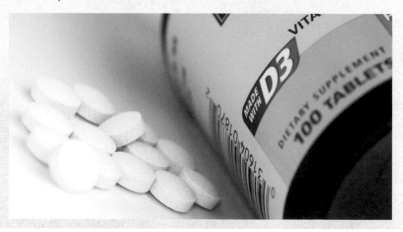

of time needed and as infrequently as possible to relieve the pain and inflammation of Crohn's disease.

Immune System Suppressors

When flare-ups occur frequently, Crohn's symptoms are moderate to severe, or anti-inflammatory drugs do not work well, doctors and patients may turn to other kinds of powerful medications —ones that work on the immune system. These are called immune system suppressors or immunomodulators. They suppress the immune system in order to weaken the inflammatory response. These drugs can heal the fistulas of Crohn's disease, keep people in remission, and relieve symptoms when corticosteroids fail. However, like all powerful drugs, they present problems.

Most of these drugs have to be injected regularly or given through an intravenous (IV) drip into a vein. They weaken the immune system so much that people are vulnerable to many infections. Even mild infections, such as colds, can be serious when taking immunomodulators, because the immune system cannot fight the infections. Jennifer, for example, caught chicken pox and had to be hospitalized for it when she was on an immune system suppressor drug. The medications can also damage the kidneys, the liver, and bone marrow, so people using these drugs have to undergo regular blood tests to be sure that the drugs are causing no harm.

Biologics

The newest types of medicines for treating Crohn's disease also work on the immune system, but instead of weakening all of it, they suppress only a specific part of the immune system. They are called biologics because they are drugs genetically engineered in a lab and made of genes, proteins, or antibodies. Infliximab is the first of these new medications. It is given to people who do not respond well to other treatments and have moderate to severe Crohn's disease. It is an antibody made from both human and mouse components that binds to a protein in the immune system called TNF-alpha. The protein is one that triggers an immune system response. Warner and Barto explain, "By targeting TNF-alpha, infliximab is able to suppress and prevent the inflammation that is the hallmark of IBD."[28] For most people infliximab works rapidly to stop flare-ups and calm the immune system inflammation, but it must be given in an IV over a six- to eight-week period, and people can become allergic to it.

No one medication is best for treating Crohn's disease, so doctors and patients need to weigh the danger and discomfort of side effects and the severity of the symptoms, consider which treatment is most effective, and reevaluate treatments regularly to maintain a good, pain-free quality of life and to stay in remission as long as possible. Most people with Crohn's are able to identify a drug treatment plan that allows them to stay symptom free for long periods of time between flare-ups and to live a healthy, normal life. Some also use antibiotics as a long-term therapy, which fights bacteria, quiets the immune system, and is especially helpful for people with recurring fistulas and abscesses. Many people with Crohn's also take antidiarrheal drugs as needed to control the frequency of diarrhea.

Diet and Stress Management

Usually, people with Crohn's disease need to combine pre-scribed medications with diet and lifestyle choices that keep their symptoms under control. Although foods do not cause Crohn's disease, they can trigger or aggravate symptoms. Different people may have difficulty with different foods and need to eliminate them from the diet. Many people, for instance, have to avoid alcohol and caffeine. Others find that fatty fried foods, dairy foods, or high-fiber foods cause problems, especially during periods of flare-ups. The staff at the Mayo Clinic says that people with Crohn's may need to eliminate from the diet any foods that are more difficult to digest, such as raw fruits and vegetables, beans, nuts, and seeds. They also recommend eating five or six small meals a day instead of three large ones.

Sometimes people with Crohn's disease have to eliminate so many healthy foods that they are in danger of becoming malnourished. People can also become malnourished from se-vere diarrhea or poor absorption of nutrients from meals.

Canadian gastroenterologist Donald R. Duerksen says that up to 80 percent of people with Crohn's disease may suffer malnutrition or weight loss. When nutrition and weight loss are a problem, vitamin and mineral supplements and diet planning with a nutritionist become a necessary part of the treatment plan. People learn to choose foods that are healthy but high in calories and are encouraged to eat snacks between meals. They are also encouraged to eat desserts. Since dehydration can be caused by frequent diarrhea, people with Crohn's also have to make an effort to drink plenty of fluids. According to University of California–San Francisco Medical Center, they must try to drink half their body weight in ounces of water. For example, a person who weighs 120 pounds (54.4kg) tries to drink 60 ounces (1.8L) of fluid per day.

Occasionally, the intestines of a person with Crohn's are so inflamed that treatment may involve resting them and temporarily going on a special, nutrition-rich liquid diet. At other

Crohn's disease sufferers may have to eliminate dairy products, high-fiber foods, raw vegetables, and nuts and seeds from their diet.

times severely inflamed intestines may be treated by not eating anything by mouth for a brief time and using special IV feedings so that the intestines can rest completely. More commonly, especially with children who are growing, high-calorie liquid nutrition supplements are prescribed along with regular meals. Nutritional treatment is very individualized. The National Digestive Diseases Information Clearinghouse (NDDIC) of the National Institutes of Health explains, "No special diet has been proven effective for preventing or treating Crohn's disease, but it is very important that people who have Crohn's disease follow a nutritious diet and avoid any foods that seem to worsen symptoms. There are no consistent dietary rules to follow that will improve a person's symptoms."[29]

Diet is but one lifestyle factor that can aggravate Crohn's disease. Another way that people with Crohn's can lessen their symptoms is by reducing stress in their lives if they discover that stress is triggering or worsening flare-ups. The staff at the Mayo Clinic says, "When you're stressed, your normal digestive process changes. Your stomach empties more slowly and secretes more acid. Stress can also speed or slow the passage of intestinal contents. It may also cause changes in intestinal tissue itself."[30] People cannot avoid all stress, but some of the treatment approaches for managing stress include exercise, deep-breathing techniques for relaxation, and yoga or meditation.

Surgical Treatment

Even with the best medical and lifestyle treatment programs, Crohn's is incurable, and over time it can cause intestinal damage that will not heal on its own. According to the National Institutes of Health, about 75 percent of people with Crohn's disease require surgery at some point in their lives. Sometimes surgery is performed to close fistulas or to drain abscesses. Sometimes a procedure called a strictureplasty is done to widen a stricture in the intestine and to remove scar tissue. Blockages may also have to be removed, and serious intestinal bleeding complications may require emergency surgery. When a section of the intestine is too damaged to repair, surgery may have to be done to remove the damaged part. The surgeon cuts the intestine above and below the diseased part and then reconnects the cut parts to form a whole, slightly shorter intestine.

In cases of severe disease, more radical surgery may be needed to allow people to live without constant symptoms and pain. The NDDIC explains, "Some people who have Crohn's disease in the large intestine need to have their entire colon removed in an operation called a colectomy. A small opening is made in the front of the abdominal wall, and the tip of the ileum, which is located at the end of the small intestine, is brought to the skin's surface." This procedure is called an ostomy. An opening, called a stoma, is made "about the size of a quarter and usually located in the right lower part of the abdomen near the beltline," says the NDDIC. "A pouch is worn over the opening to collect waste, and the patient empties the pouch as needed. The majority of colectomy patients go on to live normal, active lives."[31] Few people have such severe Crohn's that they require a colectomy and ostomy, but those who decide to have this surgery achieve freedom from living with constant pain.

Ongoing and Lifelong Treatment

Even surgical treatment, however, cannot stop the chronic disease process of Crohn's. Often the inflammation will appear in another part of the intestinal tract. About half of people who have surgery will need a second surgery, or more, in the future. Over time, medications and lifestyle adjustments may also stop working well enough to control symptoms and ongoing inflammation. That is why the Mayo Clinic says that living with Crohn's disease can be discouraging. Treatment must be lifelong and adjusted to the changing course of the disease. It cannot prevent flare-ups completely nor stop the chronic recurrence of inflammation and intestinal damage. Nevertheless, most people not only learn to cope with their disease, but manage to lead satisfying, fulfilling lives.

CHAPTER FOUR

Living with Crohn's Disease

Living with Crohn's is challenging, but people can learn to manage their symptoms and cope with this chronic disease. Whether the symptoms are mild or severe, those with Crohn's can take charge of their illness and achieve a good quality of life, even when there are many bumps in the road.

Facing Medical Challenges

The medical challenges associated with Crohn's can be hard to overcome and may severely interfere with everyday life. It is sometimes difficult for those living with the disease to accept the need for medical treatment or decide to undergo serious medical procedures. On the Crohn's & Colitis Foundation of America (CCFA) website, Lindsey, a North Carolina teen, describes a fearful challenge. She was diagnosed with Crohn's in the summer of 2008, when she was fourteen years old. She explains, "Upset and confused, I tried to ignore the fact that I had this disease. I was starting my freshman year at a new school and I didn't have time for any other distractions. However, I was unable to ignore this life-threatening disease because I experienced so many symptoms. These symptoms included experiencing discomfort, feeling extensive pain and visiting the toilet VERY often." At first Lindsey got relief from her symptoms

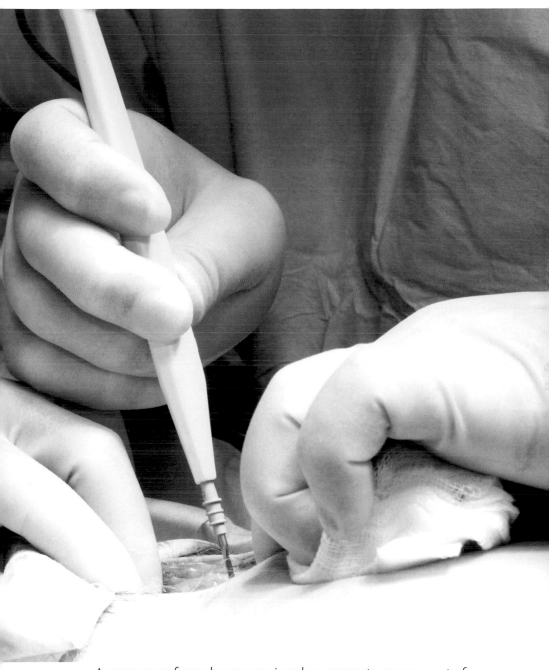

A surgeon performs laparoscopic colon surgery to remove part of a patient's lower intestine, after which the cut sections will be sewn back together.

with medications, but in the spring of the next year, she had a serious flare-up. Lindsey's doctor decided that she needed surgery. She was frightened and angry that her body had betrayed her in this way. She says, "But, I knew that in order to get well, I needed to follow through with this surgery. My doctor called it a bowel resection surgery in which a part of my terminal ileum would be cut off and sewn together to the newer, inflammation-free part of the ileum."[32]

Lindsey's resection was successful, and made a dramatic difference in her life. In 2011 she wrote, "Three years later and I am so glad that I got that surgery. Basically, I can eat anything that I want and I am so happy for that. After about the 3rd day from my surgery, I was able to eat macaroni and cheese, chicken, pudding, etc. This surgery really proved to be beneficial."[33] For people who cannot get their symptoms under control with medicine, surgery can mean living a comfortable, normal life. Lindsey tries to encourage other people with Crohn's not to let fear stop them from getting the treatment they need.

Adapting to Body-Altering Surgery

Lindsey's resection got her Crohn's symptoms under control, but sometimes people with more severe Crohn's need to undergo substantial, life-changing surgery. Facing the need for an ostomy, for example, can be traumatic. People may experience a wide range of emotions, such as anger, grief, and fear. This was the situation that twenty-four-year-old Christopher Beebe described in 2004. He suffered a rare, dangerous complication of Crohn's. His stomach and large intestine fused together and blocked off the entrance to his stomach. The only treatment that would work, doctors said, was to surgically remove the damaged parts of his intestine and stomach and to give Beebe an ileostomy. During this procedure, doctors would attach his small intestine to an opening in his abdomen where a pouch could be attached for Beebe to empty his waste. The procedure, explained the doctors, would not change much about his life; people with ileostomies can do everything—swim, play sports, live normally. The surgery just changes how they go to the bathroom. Nevertheless, accepting a pouch and ileostomy was scary.

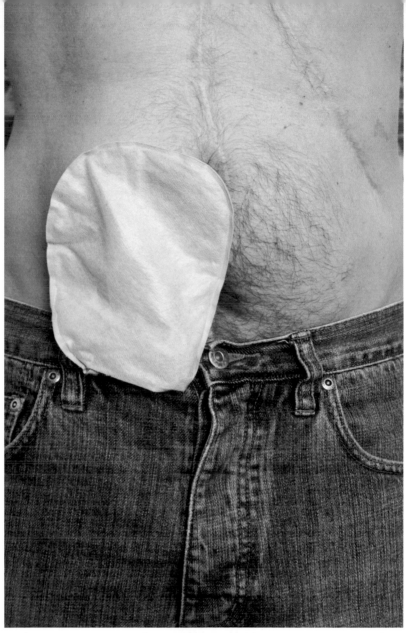

An ileostomy is a surgical procedure in which an opening is created in the ileum—the final section of the small intestine—to function as an anus. An attached pouch collects the patient's waste.

Beebe remembers, "When told of this, I thought that the rest of my life would be spent dealing with how I was different."[34]

Beebe faced the situation with courage and optimism. Almost immediately after the surgery, he began to feel better than he had in years. He says, "I always used to say that the

Being Funny

Ben Morrison is a stand-up comedian who lives in Los Angeles. He also has Crohn's disease, but instead of hiding behind a "veil of shame," he chooses to make jokes about his symptoms. He has developed a comedy routine that includes slides of intestines. Morrison makes jokes about "poop," stained underwear, and passing smelly gas. The audience laughs with him, and people with inflammatory bowel disease (IBD) appreciate the funny stories he tells. Morrison says, "I know it sounds stupid, but I don't view myself as a victim of Crohn's. I view myself as someone who has Crohn's. . . . Once you remove the stigma of talking about it, it gets kind of fun to share stories. . . . I believe in the healing role of storytelling." The name of Morrison's comedy show is "Pain in the Butt."

Quoted in Matt Kettmann. "Crohn's Disease Comedy." *Santa Barbara (CA) Independent*, February 2, 2011. www.independent.com/news/2011/feb/02/crohns-disease-comedy.

Comedian Ben Morrison's stand-up routine includes jokes about his experiences with Crohn's disease.

best thing about being sick is feeling better, and likewise, the best part about hitting bottom is that you can only rise up. . . . Every day that passed I gained a little more strength back, I could walk a little further, and breathe a little easier."[35] Since his surgery, Beebe has had no Crohn's symptoms or pain. Nothing holds him back from doing what he wants to do. He went to graduate school in engineering, and he spent a summer backpacking through Europe. He says he is healthy and happy and that his Crohn's disease has made him a stronger person. Beebe feels that he has triumphed over Crohn's.

The Ongoing Challenge of Food

Beebe managed to stay upbeat despite having to adjust to his medical emergency, but for many people the daily lifestyle demands of Crohn's disease present challenges too. Living with Crohn's can mean making radical changes in nutrition and diet and figuring out how to minimize chronic problems such as cramps, diarrhea, and pain by making the right food choices.

Matt, for example, was diagnosed with Crohn's in 1994 when he was thirteen years old. He spent his high school years coping with periodic bouts of stomach pain that developed into full flare-ups if he did not watch his diet. He learned through trial and error, he says, to avoid most flare-ups by immediately going on a liquid diet when the pain first started. He would drink the liquid nutritional supplement Ensure instead of eating meals, take pain medication, and wait for the symptoms to ease. Then, if all went well, he could move to a more normal diet. For him, the mainstays of a normal diet were foods such as beef, mashed potatoes, eggs, pasta, and breads. He had to be very careful to avoid any milk products and could eat none of his formerly favorite foods. Whenever he broke the rules of his strict diet, he would suffer a flare-up, so he had to resist temptations. Still, Matt's high school life generally went well. He says, "My life [after diagnosis] returned to a somewhat normal state. I went back to school, kept my grades up, and participated in the school choir. . . . The disease doesn't get in the way, except for when it's time to eat."[36]

Remission and Relapse

Remissions and relapses in symptoms are also an aspect of living with Crohn's that can be difficult for individuals with the disease. Throughout high school, Matt lived with good days and bad days. In 1999, however, after a bad flare-up that he could not control with a liquid diet, Matt's doctor suggested that he try the newest medication of that time. It was the biologic Remicade (infliximab). He received an intravenous (IV) infusion, and that very night, he remembers, he was free of stomach pain for the first time in four years. Remicade worked so well for him that he had his first remission from Crohn's. Carefully, he experimented with eating forbidden foods. One by one, he added French fries, barbecue sauce, yogurt, chocolate candy, and soda. His remission and dietary freedom lasted until college, when a new round of flare-ups indicated that he needed another infusion of Remicade. This worked for some months, but then Matt had a bad flare-up that would not go away, possibly aggravated by the stress of classes and exams.

Matt recovered from the severe flare-up with a liquid diet, but throughout the year, he kept suffering recurring flare-ups. Finally, he discovered why his diet efforts were not helping—his doctor found two strictures in his small intestine. At first, he tried restricting his diet even more because he did not want surgery. He remembers, "My diet consisted of a few of the same dishes, I was easily irritated, and I was relying on starch and sugar to fuel my days." In 2003 he had to give up and schedule the surgery, and slowly, as he recovered, he moved from a clear liquid diet to soft foods to a more normal diet. Matt does not complain. He controls his symptoms with diet and lifestyle adjustments as best he can, and he says, "I am living my life to the fullest."[37]

Emotional Challenges

One of the most important things Matt learned about his disease while in college is that stress aggravated his symptoms as much as diet. Many people who suffer from Crohn's have a similar experience. The National Digestive Diseases Information

People living with Crohn's disease sometimes feel increased stress and depression, which can be severely debilitating.

Clearinghouse (NDDIC) explains, "There is no evidence showing that stress causes Crohn's disease. However, people with Crohn's disease sometimes feel increased stress in their lives from having to live with a chronic illness. Some people with Crohn's disease also report that they experience a flare in disease when they are experiencing a stressful event or situation."[38]

Though stress and other emotional factors can be a significant challenge for those suffering from Crohn's, there are a variety of ways for individuals to cope with this aspect of the disease.

One mother whose son has had Crohn's since he was eight years old, for example, came to understand the debilitating effects of stress after years of struggle. Every fall, when school started, she says, her son would experience a flare-up with severe stomach cramps and pain. Though he did not appear to be experiencing stress, she believes that it was a significant factor in his flare-up. This mother writes on the CCFA website, "Now, 8 years later and a very difficult year, we have concluded that it was underlying stress (that no one was aware of) that has been the root of his pain. IF ONLY . . . his doctor would have taken me by the shoulders, shaken me and said pointedly . . . STRESS CAN ABSOLUTELY CAUSE CONSTANT PAIN."[39] For this young man, the best way to reduce stress turned out to be psychological counseling to deal with his chronic disease. With the counseling, his mother reports, this high school student is feeling much better and living a normal life.

For many people, living with Crohn's can cause not only stress but real emotional difficulties. A twenty-seven-year-old man who is a member of the CCFA explains that he struggles with depression. He believes that being honest about emotional problems and seeking the support of others is very important for people with Crohn's, whether they are experiencing typical emotional lows or are suffering from a depressive illness. He says:

> My health has been a constant battle . . . but realizing that I have depression and how that impacts my status as a person living with an autoimmune, chronic disease has been enlightening.
>
> Crohn's tugs at me every single day. Whether I'm doubled over the toilet in pain, hoping that gas is only just gas, or experiencing that all over malaise [general discomfort], this disease is one that is impeccably persistent. For me, even when I'm symptomatically in remission, my mind can't help but remind me every time I look in the mirror and see that

scar—see that disease. . . . I know it's hard to talk about
feelings sometimes, but if we can talk about how our gas
smells worse than a cow's and all the different ways feces
can look, then we can and ought to discuss how our emotional well-being is distressed by this disease.[40]

Social Challenges: Coping in the Real World

Talking about Crohn's disease or even admitting to the problems it causes can be extremely difficult for many people, both
socially and emotionally. The symptoms of Crohn's can be embarrassing, and much of society has no understanding of the
disease. The frequent, smelly diarrhea, for example, is a symptom that many people feel embarrassed about and try to keep
a secret. When the diarrhea is very frequent, people can be
afraid to leave their homes because they may need to use the
bathroom. They may avoid going out unless they know that a
bathroom will be accessible. At school or in public places, having to run to the bathroom suddenly in front of others can
make people with Crohn's feel ashamed.

Janice Chavkin, for instance, developed Crohn's in high
school and felt ashamed of her symptoms. She remembers, "I
became very withdrawn at school and stopped speaking to
everybody because I was embarrassed by what I had." When
she went to college, she was even more embarrassed by her
symptoms. She recalls rushing out of classes to get to the
bathroom and having to stay there so long that she missed
class work. Her grades dropped and she struggled academi-
cally, but she still kept her disease a secret. Today Chavkin is
no longer ashamed of her disease. She explains that Crohn's
changed her life, but she does not let it stop her from living.
She met an understanding doctor who told her no matter what
symptoms she had, she should never stop doing what she
wanted or needed to do. She took that advice to heart and
says, "If I wanted to, I could sit around and mope and cry all
day, but I'm not going to let it get there."[41] Chavkin tells everyone about her Crohn's now and has begun running marathons

Singing About Crohn's Disease

Chris Conley, singer and guitarist with the band Saves the Day, has had Crohn's disease since he was about sixteen years old. He says that sometimes, when he has flare-ups, touring can be diffi-cult. He remembers times while touring in which he had a terrible time waiting for a rest stop to use the bathroom; he has even had accidents. He also endured times when he could not eat but had to work anyway. He has coped with the side effects of many med-ications. Conley says that he has stopped being embarrassed about the symptoms of his disease. One of his songs, "Where Are You?," is about the troubles and emotions connected with Crohn's disease. He once explained about writing the song:

I have a stomach disorder called Crohn's disease and it was getting really bad when we were getting ready to tour with Weezer. I had to take steroids, which disturbs your emotional state and balance; your equilibrium is thrown off and it makes the lows lower. I happened to

be going through a sad pe-riod. The overall theme is about taking everything in, the depression, confu-sion and anxiety, but also the incredible highs.

Quoted in Music Emissions. "Saves the Day Profile Page." www.musicemissions .com/artists/Saves+The+Day.

Saves the Day's singer and guitarist Chris Conley has talked openly about his Crohn's disease, even writing the song "Where Are You?" about his experiences with the disease.

to raise money for the CCFA. She has also become an advocate for people with IBDs.

Becoming an Advocate

Ally Bain grew up with Crohn's disease, too, and she has become another advocate for people with the disease. She explains, "So many people with Crohn's disease don't talk about it—because of the symptoms and what it does to you, many people choose to be silent. But if you don't discuss it, you can't get help. By meeting others who have it, I hope I can encourage students to open up about it and get the support they need."[42] In 2004, when Bain was in high school, she was shopping with her mother when she desperately needed to use a bathroom. When she asked the store employees to allow her to use their bathroom, they refused. No one understood how important getting to a bathroom can be for someone with Crohn's. Rather than feeling ashamed, Bain and her mother discussed the situation with their representative in the state legislature and helped pass the 2005 Illinois state law named Ally's Law. It guarantees restroom access in public places to anyone with a medical emergency.

Today Bain is a college student who still fights to help people with Crohn's and to raise public awareness about the difficulties of living with the disease. She says, "I realized early on that I had to be my own advocate; my parents are loving and supportive, but they can't always be there. Now, I'm politically active, speaking publicly about the issues that affect people with inflammatory bowel disease."[43]

Telling the World, Admitting the Problems

By speaking openly and honestly about their problems, people with Crohn's both educate others and help themselves. Matt, for example, once brought extra Ensure to the cafeteria for all his friends to taste at lunch. He explains the benefits of this by saying, "They get to experience what we have to drink during our liquid diet phases, and you get satisfaction of knowing that your friends know a little bit more about what it's like to live with the disease."[44] He decided not to keep his disease a secret from college administrators and faculty either. He registered with the university disability office, which meant that letters were sent to all his class professors. They were informed that he might miss classes due to illness or be unable to get assignments finished on time. The professors were willing to work with Matt to adapt their requirements to his condition.

Megan, a Canadian college student, got support from her university's office for students with disabilities, too. The staff made special arrangements for her to take exams apart from other students because the stress always aggravated her symptoms. Megan explains, "I used to worry about my stomach and diarrhea during exams. Now, I have my own exam room with a bathroom nearby and I can get up as many times as I need to. My last two midterms were the best exams I've ever written! And if I'm sick with a flare-up, someone will even take class notes for me." Megan's friends are understanding and helpful. They accept the fact that she can never drink alcohol. Her roommates are willing to join her in making and eating Crohn's-friendly meals. Megan's university adviser even helped students with IBD to form a support group so they could get to know each other and share experiences. In high school Megan was embarrassed by her Crohn's disease, but that is no longer the case. She says, "A huge place in my heart has opened up to spread awareness and share with others about digestive disease."[45]

Finding Support

Support groups help many people with Crohn's adjust to life with a chronic disease. Like Megan, many people find understanding and self-acceptance by joining a support group. The CCFA, for example, offers more than three hundred local support groups around the United States in which people with IBDs and their family members can meet with others struggling with the same diseases. As the members of the groups get to know each other, they share their problems, gain practical coping information, and encourage each other to live normal, fulfilling lives. Children and teens often benefit from supportive environments, too. The CCFA provides twelve camps for

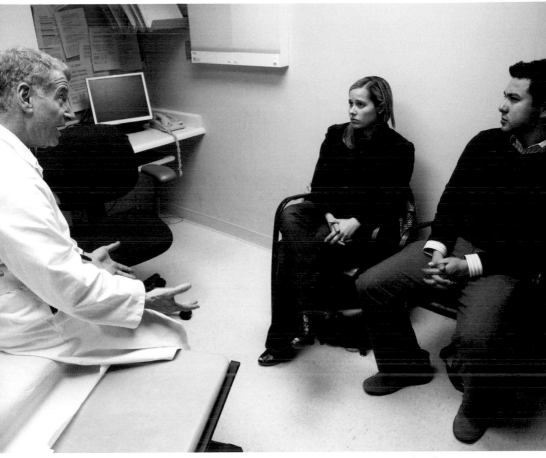

When a Crohn's patient consults with a physician about the disease, the doctor typically discusses treatment options, as well as support groups that may help in coping with the disease.

children with IBD so that they can experience typical summer fun while receiving appropriate medical care. The camps, in different locations in the United States, are named Camp Oasis and are often staffed by counselors who have IBD and were former campers themselves. The CCFA says campers find friends who accept them, and they gain confidence as they share their difficulties with people who understand them.

One young camper says, "Without Camp Oasis I don't think I would be comfortable having Crohn's disease at all. I know I definitely wouldn't be open about it, and by meeting all these other kids just like me, I've learned that it's okay to be different and people will just accept me for who I am, and if they don't, then they aren't worth it."[46] A Camp Oasis counselor adds, "To me, Camp Oasis means that we can show a lot of kids that they are not the only one with IBD, and that despite having IBD they can still do whatever they want."[47] Living with Crohn's does not mean that the disease has to run a person's life. Even young people can learn to believe in themselves and take control of their lives.

CHAPTER FIVE

The Future of Crohn's Disease

Danielle Desbiens of Quebec, Ontario, Canada, has had Crohn's disease for more than thirty years. She is an active fund-raiser and community advocate for the Crohn's and Colitis Foundation of Canada (CCFC). She works to support the CCFC's ongoing mission to fund inflammatory bowel disease (IBD) medical research. She explains, "I am there to find a cure so I can help others and their families live a long and healthy life."[48]

Research Needed

The CCFC website states that a cure for Crohn's and ulcerative colitis can and will be found, and to that end it works to raise funds for medical research. The U.S. counterpart of the CCFC, the Crohn's & Colitis Foundation of America (CCFA), has a similar goal. Its website says, "Our Mission: To cure Crohn's disease and ulcerative colitis, and to improve the quality of life of children and adults affected by these diseases."[49] Since it was established in 1967, the CCFA has contributed more than $150 million to medical research on the treatment and cure of IBD. For example, the CCFA provided a grant to the researchers who discovered the NOD2 gene that is correlated with Crohn's disease.

The CCFA explains, however, that despite significant scientific advances, many research challenges remain. Scientists

Hundreds of runners await the start of the Zappos.com Rock 'n' Roll Las Vegas Marathon in December 2010, which benefits the Crohn's and Colitis Foundation of America. The organization's objectives include raising money for research and improving the quality of life for people with IBD.

and medical doctors still do not know the cause of Crohn's disease. They cannot predict who will develop Crohn's, and they have no medicine to prevent it in people who are genetically or environmentally vulnerable. They do not know what treatments will ensure that all patients achieve remission. They cannot prevent relapses or prevent complications such as fistulas, obstructions, and abscesses. The need to deal with these issues and to address unanswered questions about IBD is a driving motivation behind medical research all over the world. Ultimately, researchers hope, their increased knowledge will lead to a cure.

Genetic Research

In the effort to understand the causes of Crohn's, some scientists concentrate on genes and the immune system, while others examine environmental triggers. At the University of Pittsburgh and its IBD Center, for example, researchers Richard H. Duerr and Arthur M. Barrie received a grant from the CCFA in 2011 to study how genes that direct immune system reactions may lead to the development of IBD. The scientists believe that some genes that code for a specific immune

Scientists believe that some genes that code for a specific immune system cell—the helper T cell (purple)—may be defective in people with IBD.

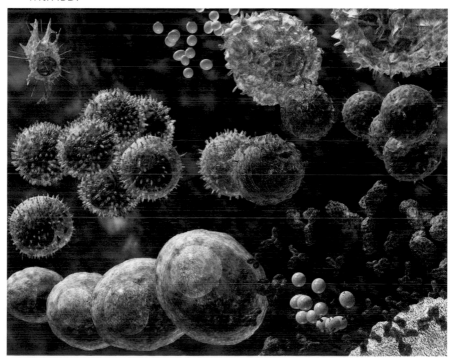

system cell—the helper T cell—may be defective in people with IBD. The helper T cell, according to immune system expert Lauren Sompayrac, "serves as the quarterback of the immune system team. It directs the action by secreting protein molecules called cytokines."[50] These cytokine factories tell all the other immune system cells when and how to respond to an invader. Variants in genes that direct the functioning of helper T cells may affect how the whole immune system works.

Duerr and Barrie theorize that the genes that code for a particular kind of helper T cell, called Th17, do not work correctly in individuals with Crohn's. Instead, defective genes allow immune system fighters to injure the intestines uncontrollably, resulting in an autoimmune disease. Barrie explains, "Patients with IBD have excessive numbers of Th17 cells in their inflamed intestines, and we believe that the presence of these cells perpetuates IBD."[51] The scientists want to figure out exactly why too many Th17 helper T cells are found in the inflamed intestines, how they cause the inflammation, and which genes are responsible. Duerr and Barrie are just beginning their research, but they believe that understanding gene variations and the effects on Th17 cells could someday lead to developing new treatments for intestinal diseases.

Blocking Immune System Errors

At Cornell University's College of Veterinary Medicine, researchers Eric Denkers and Charlotte Egan are studying immune system cells, too, in the hope that they will find new treatments for Crohn's disease. The scientists were studying a parasite called toxoplasma and how it infects mice when they realized that infected mice had the same symptoms as people with Crohn's disease. The discovery made them turn their research toward understanding what causes the inflammation, in the hopes that discovering the root cause in mice would illuminate how Crohn's is developed in humans. In mice with toxoplasma infections, some immune system cells in the intestines accumulate excessively, overreact, and cause inflammation. These cells, called intraepithelial lymphocytes, cause the mice to show symptoms similar to those seen with Crohn's disease.

Hookworms to the Rescue?

At the University of Nottingham in England, Christopher Hawkey and his research team are conducting a study to see if hookworm infections are a good treatment for Crohn's disease. Hookworms are intestinal parasites. They cling to the intestinal walls with little hooks and feed on blood. Hookworms live successfully inside the intestine because, like other parasites, they excrete chemicals that suppress the immune system and prevent an inflammatory response. This protects them from being attacked as foreign invaders. Researchers believe that this effect might also quiet an overactive immune system. Hookworm infections have already been shown to reduce the symptoms of allergies and asthma. Hawkey and his team theorize that hookworms may have similar effects on those with Crohn's disease. As part of their study, they are deliberately infecting volunteers with the eggs, or larvae, of hookworms to determine if the infections have anti-inflammatory results. The trial, begun in 2006, is still ongoing, but the researchers say, "This study is worth conducting because primarily it will investigate an exciting new therapy.... We believe that providing insight to the interaction of the environment (i.e. parasites) and immune response, with the hope of new therapeutic strategies, is a core need for these patients."

P.J. Fortun, D. Pritchard, J. Britton, J.S. Sithole, A. Cole, and C.J. Hawkey. "Hookworm Infestation as Therapy in Crohn's Disease." Protocol document, version 2.2 (23.03.06), University of Nottingham, p. 12.

Computer artwork shows hookworms embedded in the walls of the intestine. The worms excrete chemicals that suppress the immune system and prevent an inflammatory response.

Denkers and Egan also had a strain of mice that were resistant to toxoplasma infection. Even when exposed to the parasite, the mice did not get sick. Egan says, "We found this profound increase of intraepithelial lymphocytes in the diseased animal, but not in the resistant animal. So what we've been doing is isolating these cells and trying to better understand their function."[52]

The scientists do not believe that Crohn's disease is caused by a parasite. But they do think that variations in the immune system can cause too many intraepithelial lymphocytes to swarm to the site of an infection. When the immune system is unable to generate an excess of the cells, then no inflammation occurs. Using their mice subjects, Denkers and Egan want to figure out a way to block the immune system from producing intraepithelial lymphocytes. If they succeed, the researchers hope to develop a way to treat intestinal inflammation or prevent it altogether. Then, someday, they might be able to create a treatment that prevents the inflammation in humans.

Probiotics Research

Laboratory experiments are usually the first step in understanding human diseases. In 2011, for example, at Northwestern University, Mansour Mohamadzadeh and his research team used mice to test a new IBD treatment. Based on information gathered from prior research, the scientists decided to study the value of probiotics for treating intestinal inflammation in their mice. Probiotics are live bacteria or other microorganisms that resemble the friendly bacteria and microorganisms living in human and animal intestinal tracts. Scientists have evidence that probiotics can improve digestive health by preventing the invasion of infecting bacteria. They may also help the immune system to function normally. One kind of probiotic is called *Lactobacillus acidophilus*. It is a bacterium commonly found in yogurt. This was the probiotic studied by Mohamadzadeh and his team. Even friendly bacteria may cause a reaction in defective immune systems, so the scientists removed the antigens on the cell surfaces of the bacteria before giving the probiotics to the mice. They did this by deleting the gene that codes for the development of antigens. This meant that the immune systems

The bacterium *Lactobacillus acidophilus,* which is present in yogurt, may be an effective probiotic to treat Crohn's.

in the mouse subjects would not generate any antibodies, and the bacteria were safe for inflamed intestines.

In the laboratory the researchers fed the genetically changed *Lactobacillus acidophilus* to mice that had two different types of ulcerative colitis that are similar to this form of IBD in humans. After thirteen days of consuming the probiotics, 95 percent of the mice had almost no inflammation in their colons. Mohamadzadeh explains that the probiotics acted like a peacekeeping force and soothed the overactive immune system cells in the colon. He says:

> They essentially calm everything down and restore it to normal. This opens brand new avenues to treat various autoimmune diseases of the gut, including inflammatory bowel disease and colon cancer, all of which can be triggered by imbalanced inflammatory immune response. Such gene targeting in a probiotic bacteria such as Lactobacillus acidophilus offers the possibility of a safe, drug-free treatment in the near future.[53]

The next step for the researchers is to test the treatment in humans. The team hopes that they have discovered a new, powerful treatment for people with IBD. If they are right, the

Gut Types

In April 2011 an international research team led by Jeroen Raes of the University of Brussels reported discovering that there are three different categories of bacteria that can be predominant in an individual's intestinal tract. The researchers call these different groups "gut types." This means that each person has an intestinal system of a particular type, depending on the most common type of bacteria that live there. The three types are named for the kinds of bacteria. They are *Bacteroides*, *Prevotella*, and *Ruminococcus*. All of them are normal, but the gut type of a particular individual, say the researchers, can determine how he or she digests and uses food. The researchers believe that it can also determine which medicine works best for which person. Different gut types could explain why some medicines work well for one person with Crohn's but not for others or why some cause adverse side effects. Raes says that someday the best treatment and dose of medicine for diseases might be determined by the person's gut type. The researchers do not yet know if gut types can change over a person's lifetime or how to adjust treatment to gut type, but their discovery may lead to personalized treatment decisions for Crohn's in the future.

genetically altered probiotics may even be able to prevent the flare-ups and relapses that are so common with Crohn's disease.

Antibiotics Research

Thomas J. Borody, a gastroenterologist in Australia, believes that he has already found the best treatment for Crohn's disease. He is one of the scientists who believe that Crohn's is caused by *Mycobacterium avium* subspecies *paratuberculosis* (MAP) infections. His company, Giaconda, has developed a combination antibiotic (three antibiotics in one medicine) named

Myoconda to heal Crohn's by killing the infecting bacteria. In trials involving long-term treatment with the drug in Australia, Borody and his colleagues report healing of inflammation and remission of Crohn's symptoms. However, the remissions did not last any longer than the remissions experienced by people getting other kinds of medications for Crohn's. Borody's team is studying the benefits of increasing the doses of Myoconda in new research efforts because they believe that they are attacking the cause of Crohn's and can eventually cure it. In England John Hermon-Taylor continues his research into MAP as the cause of Crohn's and has developed a vaccine, but it has not been tested in people yet. Researchers who believe that MAP causes Crohn's disease often have a difficult time getting the funds to test their treatments because many in the scientific community oppose the controversial theory and do not support the research. No one really knows today if antibiotics or a vaccine can cure Crohn's disease by healing MAP infections.

The Crohn's Disease Initiative, established by microbiologist Rod Chiodini, is an organization of scientists and others who believe that the controversy about MAP and Crohn's disease must be settled. In association with the University of Texas–El Paso, Texas Tech University Health Sciences Center, and private sponsors, the organization seeks to raise money to support scientific research that will determine if MAP is the cause of some cases of Crohn's disease. The Crohn's Disease Initiative has set a goal of a five-year plan to study human subjects and prove or disprove that MAP infection is the cause of Crohn's— at least some of the time. It says that researchers must first identify people with MAP in their intestinal tissue, then treat the infection, and finally monitor whether the reduction of bacteria results in improvement of inflammation. The trials would have to show that MAP is always or usually associated with Crohn's disease—that when the infection occurs, the disease occurs. However, says Chiodini, "There is a BIG difference between association and causality, and until causality is directly addressed, the controversy will continue. . . . My intent is to bring objectivity and focus back into the field with the goal of either dismissing or establishing a causative role of this agent—this controversy has continued for too long!"[54] If the Crohn's Disease Initiative is successful in its plans, the researchers will know whether MAP causes Crohn's or is just an incidental infection that does no harm. If they find that it can cause Crohn's, they will have a treatment answer for many infected people.

New Medicines on the Way

Many in the medical community are searching for treatments that address autoimmune disease and the symptoms that Crohn's causes. The pharmaceutical companies GlaxoSmith-Kline and ChemoCentryx have developed a new medication for Crohn's that is currently being tested in people. For now, it is called GSK1605786. It is designed to block the movement of B cells and T cells into the intestinal tract and thus reduce inflammation. Since the drug blocks only these activated B cells and T cells, it does not suppress the whole immune system as do current immunomodulators.

The trials of the new drug will examine its safety and determine if it can induce remission of inflammation and other symptoms. In laboratory mice the drug worked well to reduce inflammation, and it did the same in small groups of human test volunteers. Among these human volunteers, after one year of treatment, 47 percent were in remission. This compares to only 31 percent given a fake pill called a placebo; it was significant evidence that the drug was effective. Also, in the group given a placebo, only 28 percent maintained remission without the use of corticosteroid treatment. Of the people given GSK1605786, 41 percent were in remission without needing any corticosteroids. These results suggest that the new medicine will help people avoid current medicines that cause uncomfortable side effects. Now, in the last trial involving a large number of people with Crohn's, researchers plan to enroll about twenty-five hundred people to test the new drug during 2011. If all goes well, the pharmaceutical companies expect to be able to introduce the drug in 2017.

Crohn's disease researchers are dedicated to finding new treatments that are safer and more comfortable for people than the medicines used today. Explains Hamed Laroui, a researcher at Emory University in Atlanta, Georgia, "A major advance in therapeutic strategies in diseases such as IBD would be the ability to target drugs to the site of the inflammation in sufficient quantities to maximize local drug concentration and minimize systemic [system-wide] side effects."[55] To this end, researchers at Emory University have developed nanoparticles (microscopic particles) that can deliver anti-inflammatory medicines directly to the intestinal tract. They tested the nanoparticles in mice with ulcerative colitis and successfully targeted the inflammation in the mice. Someday, the researchers hope that this delivery system can be used to treat people with IBD, too. Ideally, this method would carry safe, low doses of anti-inflammatory medicine to the intestinal tract of people with IBD and relieve their symptoms without affecting any other parts of their bodies or causing any side effects.

Stem Cell Therapy: The Ultimate Answer?

It will be years before nanoparticle therapy is available to people with Crohn's disease, because the research is just beginning. Treatment of Crohn's is constantly evolving, however, and several new treatments are being tested by researchers around the world. At the University of Chicago, physician David T. Rubin says, "We are extremely optimistic about new treatments that are coming and look forward to more effective and safe therapies in the near future."[56] In 2010 Rubin said that there were at least twenty new drugs being investigated and tested as improved treatments for Crohn's disease. Still, these medicines are treatments, not cures, and finding a cure is the ultimate goal for Crohn's. Many scientists do believe that a cure is possible. One idea for a cure that is being explored by researchers involves the use of stem cells.

Stem cells are the body's master cells from which all other cells are formed. They are unique cells that are unspecialized—they do not perform a specific function like heart cells or immune system cells. However, they are able to differentiate—to become specialized cells—and then to divide and multiply. Stem cells are the way that the body repairs itself, replaces injured or dead cells, and generates new functioning cells. In the bone marrow, in the centers of bones, are stem cells named hematopoietic stem cells. They generate, or give rise to, eight different kinds of new blood cells, including the white blood cells of the immune system. Most stem cells are in a resting state most of the time, but hematopoietic stem cells are turned on and active. This is true because the blood cells are short-lived and must be continually replaced. It is these hematopoietic stem cells that gastroenterologist Christopher Hawkey of Nottingham University in Great Britain is using to try to cure Crohn's disease.

One treatment being explored by researchers investigating Crohn's disease is the use of stem cells to "reboot" the immune system by extracting bone marrow, preserving it in the laboratory, and then reimplanting the marrow in the patient.

In 2007 Hawkey and his research team began a long-term trial, using stem cells to treat volunteers throughout Europe who have severe Crohn's disease. The researchers are trying to "reboot" the immune system in these people using stem cell transplants. The treatment involves extracting bone marrow stem cells and preserving them in the laboratory. Then the patient's own active immune system cells are killed—poisoned in the same way that doctors kill cancer cells with chemotherapy. Finally, the preserved stem cells from the patient's body are transplanted back into the patient's body, where they specialize into new immune system cells.

The theory behind this treatment is that the Crohn's patient's immune cells, already genetically coded to respond to an environmental trigger, have been "taught" to overreact and cause an inflammatory autoimmune disease. The stem cells from the bone marrow, still unspecialized and undifferentiated, have not "learned" to cause autoimmune disease because they have never been exposed to the environmental trigger. The transplant is a way to let the person start over, with an immune system in the state it was before the environmental trigger happened. Hawkey says, "People with severe Crohn's have very poor quality of life and at the moment there is no cure for them. So what we are attempting to achieve with this trial is something really quite radical and ambitious—and [that] could make a major difference to the lives of a lot of patients."[57]

Hawkey's team has named their study the Autologous Stem Cell Transplant International Crohn's Disease Trial (ASTIC). ("Autologous" refers to using the person's own stem cells instead of a donor's for the stem cell transplant.) By the end of 2010, ASTIC had treated only about seventeen patients with transplants, and it is still enrolling volunteers for the trial. Undergoing the treatment is not easy. The process is painful and difficult and takes about two years. Even when the trial is completed, the results will have to be analyzed, and patients will have to be followed for a long time to be sure that the stem cells have done their jobs. However, says, Hawkey, "I'm hopeful that half or more of the patients who undergo stem cell transplantation may either be cured or have a long-term remission."[58]

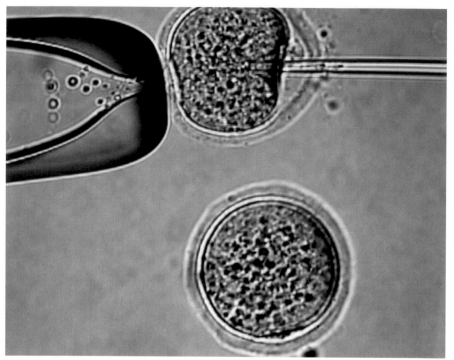

This light micrograph shows a mouse egg cell held by a pipette. Laboratory experiments with the genetic material in animal cells may be the first step in developing genetically-based treatments for Crohn's disease in the future.

Toward a Bright, Hopeful Future

Stem cell treatment for Crohn's is very new, but efforts to develop different stem cell treatments for the disease are ongoing around the world. Many scientists and medical researchers believe that research such as Hawkey's will lead to cures or vastly improved therapies in just a few years. Wherever the answers come from, most Crohn's experts believe that new breakthroughs in treatments and therapies are near. Say Warner and Barto, "The past 10 to 15 years have witnessed great strides in understanding the basic immunology of IBD and dramatic advances in the treatment of IBD. With this strong foundation to grow upon, the future for individuals with IBD is both bright and hopeful."[59]

Notes

Introduction: The Challenge of Crohn's Disease

1. Quoted in Annette Racond. "Field of Dreams: Jacksonville Jaguars' Quarterback David Garrard Tackles Crohn's." Crohn's & Colitis Foundation of America, December 2, 2005. www.ccfa.org/about/news/garrard.
2. Quoted in Ilyssa Panitz. "NFL Star David Garrard on Battling Crohn's Disease and How He's Helping Kids with the Illness." ParentDish, January 11, 2011. www.parentdish.com/2011/01/10/david-garrard-on-crohns-disease-and-becoming-a-voice-for-the-ca.
3. Quoted in Panitz. "NFL Star David Garrard on Battling Crohn's Disease and How He's Helping Kids with the Illness."

Chapter One: What Is Crohn's Disease?

4. "Early Stages: Bathing Suit." IBD Experience Journal, Children's Hospital Boston. www.experiencejournal.com/ibd/child_earlystages.shtml.
5. Alex's Mother. "IBD story." Growing Up IBD, September 2005. www.growingupibd.org/alex.
6. Andrew S. Warner and Amy E. Barto. *100 Questions and Answers About Crohn's Disease and Ulcerative Colitis: A Lahey Clinic Guide*. Sudbury, MA: Jones and Bartlett, 2007, p. 5.
7. Quoted in Warner and Barto. *100 Questions and Answers About Crohn's Disease and Ulcerative Colitis*, p. 11.
8. Quoted in Warner and Barto. *100 Questions and Answers About Crohn's Disease and Ulcerative Colitis*, p. 83.
9. Mayo Clinic Staff. "Crohn's Disease: Complications." Mayo Clinic, August 8, 2009. www.mayoclinic.com/health/crohns-disease/DS00104/DSECTION=complications.

10. David B. Sachar and Aaron E. Walfish. "Crohn's Disease." Merck Manuals Online Medical Library, August, 2006. www.merckmanuals.com/home/ag/sec09/ch126/ch126b.html.

Chapter Two: The Cause of Crohn's Disease

11. Quoted in Gina Roberts-Grey. "The Big News on Crohn's: Cynthia McFadden's Story." Celebrity Health Minute, November 8, 2010. http://celebrityhealthminute.com/2010/11/08/the-big-news-on-crohns-cynthia-mcfaddens-story.

12. Warner and Barto. *100 Questions and Answers About Crohn's Disease and Ulcerative Colitis*, p. 6.

13. Lauren Sompayrac. *How the Immune System Works*. 3rd ed. Malden, MA: Blackwell, 2008, p. 106.

14. James Byrne and Thomas Tu. "Crohn's Disease—Your Body Hates Your Guts." *Disease of the Week!*, WordPress.com, February 6, 2010. http://diseaseoftheweek.wordpress.com/2010/02/06/crohn%E2%80%99s-disease-%E2%80%93-your-body-hates-your-guts.

15. Quoted in University of Chicago Medical Center. "Researchers Find First Gene That Increases Risk of Crohn's Disease." *ScienceDaily*, May 24 2001. www.sciencedaily.com/releases/2001/05/010522073543.htm.

16. Quoted in McGill University. "Gene That Increases Susceptibility to Crohn's Disease Discovered." *ScienceDaily*, January 10, 2009. www.sciencedaily.com/releases/2009/01/090108144755.htm.

17. Warner and Barto. *100 Questions and Answers About Crohn's Disease and Ulcerative Colitis*, p. 174.

18. Jean-Paul Achkar. "Inflammatory Bowel Disease." American College of Gastroenterology. www.acg.gi.org/patients/gihealth/ibd.asp.

19. Rita Baron-Faust and Jill P. Buyon. *The Autoimmune Connection: Essential Information for Women on Diagnosis, Treatment, and Getting On with Your Life*. New York: McGraw-Hill, 2003, p. 200.

20. John Hermon-Taylor. "MAP Doomsday." Chronic Crohn's Campaign UK, CommuniGate, August 2009. www.communigate.co.uk/sussex/thechroniccrohnscampaignuk/page75.phtml.

21. L. Campbell Levy and Kim L. Isaacs. "MAPping the Cause of Crohn's Disease or Simply Along for the Ride?" *Practical Gastroenterology*, March 2008, p. 21. www.practical gastro.com/pdf/March08/PG_Mar08LevyArticle.pdf.

22. Natalie A. Molodecky and Gilaad G. Kaplan. "Environmental Risk Factors for Inflammatory Bowel Disease." *Gastroenterology & Hepatology*, May 2010, p. 344. www.clinical advances.com/article_pdfs/gh-article-201005-kaplan.pdf.

Chapter Three: Diagnosis and Treatment of Crohn's Disease

23. Mayo Clinic Staff. "Crohn's Disease: Treatments and Diagnosis." www.mayoclinic.com/health/crohns-disease/DS 00104/DSECTION=tests-and-diagnosis.

24. Mayo Clinic. "Gastrointestinal Bleeding: Diagnosis." www .mayoclinic.org/gastrointestinal-bleeding/diagnosis.html.

25. Mayo Clinic Staff. "Crohn's Disease: Treatments and Drugs." Mayo Clinic. www.mayoclinic.com/health/crohns-disease/DS00104/DSECTION=treatments-and-drugs.

26. Crohn's & Colitis Foundation of America. "Aminosalicylates: Treatment." www.ccfa.org/info/treatment/aminosalicylates.

27. Quoted in Warner and Barto. *100 Questions and Answers About Crohn's Disease and Ulcerative Colitis*, p. 42.

28. Warner and Barto. *100 Questions and Answers About Crohn's Disease and Ulcerative Colitis*, p. 48.

29. National Digestive Diseases Information Clearinghouse. "Crohn's Disease." February 2006. http://digestive.niddk.nih .gov/ddiseases/pubs/crohns.

30. Mayo Clinic Staff. "Crohn's Disease: Lifestyle and Home Remedies." Mayo Clinic. www.mayoclinic.com/health/crohns-disease/DS00104/DSECTION=lifestyle-and-home-remedies.

31. National Digestive Diseases Information Clearinghouse. "Crohn's Disease."

Chapter Four : Living with Crohn's Disease

32. Lindsey. "Resection Surgery." Crohn's and Colitis Community, Crohn's & Colitis Foundation of America, February 23, 2011. www.ccfacommunity.org/Story.aspx?storyid=869.

33. Lindsey. "Resection Surgery."
34. Quoted in *Lahey Clinic*. "Living with Crohn's Disease." Spring 2004, p. 17. www.lahey.org/Search.aspx?searchtext= crohn's%20beebe.
35. Quoted in *Lahey Clinic*. "Living with Crohn's Disease."
36. Matt the Webmaster. "My Life with Crohn's Disease." Teens with Crohn's, June 2003. http://pages.prodigy.net/matt green/abothost.htm.
37. Matt the Webmaster. "My Life with Crohn's Disease."
38. National Digestive Diseases Information Clearinghouse. "Crohn's Disease."
39. Kiptak. "Stress and Crohn's." Crohn's and Colitis Community, Crohn's and Colitis Foundation of America, December 21, 2010. www.ccfacommunity.org/Story.aspx?storyid= 842.
40. Amkraft. "Crohn's, Stones, and Feeling Blue." Crohn's and Colitis Community, Crohn's and Colitis Foundation of America, November 27, 2010. www.ccfacommunity.org/ Story.aspx?storyid=836.
41. Quoted in Diana Rodriguez. "Living with Crohn's Disease: Janice's Story." Everyday Health, September 2, 2010. www .everydayhealth.com/crohns-disease/janices-story.aspx.
42. Ally Bain. "After 3 Crohn's Disease Surgeries, I'm Finally in Remission." Health.com, March 8, 2010. www.health .com/health/condition-article/0,,20349593_1,00.html.
43. Bain. "After 3 Crohn's Disease Surgeries, I'm Finally in Remission."
44. Matt the Webmaster. "My Life with Crohn's Disease."
45. Quoted in Canadian Digestive Health Foundation. "Accepting the Journey to a Happier Gut—and Soul." www.cdhf.ca/ pdfs/stories/CDHF_PersonalStory_CrohnsIBS_MH.pdf#zoom =100.
46. Quoted in Crohn's & Colitis Foundation of America. "Camper Voices." January 9, 2009. www.ccfa.org/kids teens/testimonials/campers.
47. Quoted in Crohn's & Colitis Foundation of America. "Counselor Voices." January 9, 2009. www.ccfa.org/kidsteens/testi monials/counselors.

Chapter Five: The Future of Crohn's Disease

48. Quoted in Crohn's and Colitis Foundation of Canada. "Personal Stories: Real People." www.ccfc.ca/site/c.ajIRK4NLLh J0E/b.6349451/k.C759/Personal_Stories_Real_People.htm.

49. Crohn's & Colitis Foundation of America. "About the Crohn's & Colitis Foundation." August 5, 2008. www.ccfa .org/about/?LMI=0.

50. Sompayrac. *How the Immune System Works*, p. 8.

51. Quoted in University of Pittsburgh Medical Center (UPMC). "Pitt and UPMC Researchers Receive Grant to Study Genetic Links to Inflammatory Bowel Disease." News release, February 7, 2011. www.upmc.com/MediaRelations/News Releases/2011/Pages/Pitt-UPMC-Researchers-Receive-Grant-to-Study-Genetic-Links-to-IBD.aspx.

52. Quoted in Rebecca Harris. "Parasite May Help Crohn's Disease Research." *Cornell Daily Sun*, April 7, 2011. http:// cornellsun.com/section/news/content/2011/04/07/parasite-may-help-crohn%E2%80%99s-disease-research.

53. Quoted in Marla Paul. "New Probiotic Combats Inflammatory Bowel Disease." Northwestern University, January 31, 2011. www.northwestern.edu/newscenter/stories/2011/01/ probiotic-inflammatory-bowel-disease.html.

54. Rod Chiodini. "A Message from Dr. Chiodini." Crohn's Disease Initiative: Solving the Crohn's Disease-MAP Controversy. www.thecrohnsdiseaseinitiative.com/message.php.

55. Quoted in *Digestive Disease News*, "Drug-Loaded Nanoparticles May Offer Precise Targeting in Treatment of Inflammatory Bowel Disease." Winter 2011. www.digestive.niddk .nih.gov/about/DDnews/Win11/3.htm.

56. David T. Rubin. "For Our Patients: Living with Crohn's Disease; Five Facts for Patients & Families." Rubin Group, University of Chicago. http://drubin.bsd.uchicago.edu/patients/ crohnsdisease/livingwithcrohns.html.

57. Quoted in University of Nottingham. "Could Stem Cells Be Used to Cure Crohn's Disease?" *ScienceDaily*, December 3, 2007. www.sciencedaily.com/releases/2007/11/071130223 834.htm.

58. Quoted in Denis Campbell. "Stem Cell Treatment Gives Hope to Crohn's Disease Sufferers." *Guardian* (UK), June 23, 2009. www.guardian.co.uk/science/2009/jun/23/stem-cell-treatment-crohns-disease.

59. Warner and Barto. *100 Questions and Answers About Crohn's Disease and Ulcerative Colitis*, p. 192.

Glossary

abscesses: Walled-off collections of pus with swelling and inflammation around them.

antibodies: Proteins produced by the immune system that mark foreign invaders for destruction.

antigens: Any substances that generate the production of antibodies.

anus: The opening through which waste is eliminated from the body.

autoimmune disease: A disease in which the immune system attacks a part of the body as if it were a foreign invader. The body turns on and attacks itself, producing antibodies against its own tissues.

bowel: Another word for intestine.

colon: The major portion of the large intestine, which extends to the rectum.

dehydration: The loss of water and the essential salts required for normal body function; dehydration occurs when the body loses more fluids than it takes in.

endoscopy: A medical procedure for visual examination of the inside of any hollow organ such as the small intestine or the colon.

fistulas: Tunnels or passageways caused by sores or ulcers that connect two organs of the body, different parts of the intestine, or an organ with the outside of the body.

flare-ups: Periods during which a disease is active and causing symptoms; recurring episodes of uncontrolled inflammation.

gastrointestinal (GI): Relating to the stomach and intestines.

genes: Discrete segments of DNA that code for specific units of inheritance.

inflammation: A reaction of body tissues to injury that includes redness, swelling, heat, pain, and loss of function.

IBD: Inflammatory bowel disease; a chronic disorder of the intestinal tract. Crohn's disease and ulcerative colitis are the two most common inflammatory bowel diseases.

immune system: The complex system of cells, tissues, and organs that differentiates between self and nonself and protects the body from foreign substances and disease.

immunomodulators: Medications that suppress or diminish immune system functions.

intestine: The section of the digestive tract from the stomach to the anus. In humans the intestine is divided into two parts—the small intestine and the large intestine.

nanoparticles: Ultrafine particles that are 100 nanometers or less in size. (A nanometer is one-billionth of a meter.)

ostomy: A surgical procedure that creates an artificial opening (a stoma) for the elimination of waste from the body.

rectum: The end of the large intestine, which is connected to the anus. It holds and stores waste until it is eliminated.

remissions: Periods during which a chronic disease and its symptoms partially or completely disappear.

strictures: Narrowing in the intestines caused by scar tissue from prolonged inflammation.

Organizations to Contact

American College of Gastroenterology
PO Box 342260
Bethesda, MD 20827-2260
Phone: (301) 263-9000
Website: www.acg.gi.org

The American College of Gastroenterology is an international professional organization dedicated to advancing medical treatments and the study of gastrointestinal diseases. It also provides educational information for patients and their families.

Canadian Digestive Health Foundation
1500 Upper Middle Rd., Unit 3
PO Box 76059
Oakville, ON L6M 3H5
Phone: (905) 829-3949
Website: www.cdhf.ca/main.php

This Canadian charitable organization's mission is to provide advice and support for people with digestive diseases. At its website, people can gather educational information, ask questions of a medical expert, and share experiences with others who have digestive diseases.

Crohn's & Colitis Foundation of America (CCFA)
386 Park Ave. S., 17th Fl.
New York, NY 10016
Phone: (800) 932-2423
E-mail: info@ccfa.org
Website: www.ccfa.org

The CCFA is a nonprofit organization dedicated to finding a cure for Crohn's disease and ulcerative colitis. It funds research, supports a scientific journal, and provides education and support for people with inflammatory bowel disease (IBD), their families, and friends.

National Digestive Diseases Information Clearinghouse (NDDIC)
2 Information Way
Bethesda, MD 20892-3570
Phone: (800) 891-5389
E-mail: nddic@info.niddk.nih.gov
Website: http://digestive.niddk.nih.gov

The NDDIC is a service of the National Institute of Diabetes and Digestive and Kidney Diseases of the U.S. National Institutes of Health. It provides educational information, information on ongoing clinical trials, and a newsletter about digestive diseases for the general public and health care professionals.

Ostomy Support Groups
United Ostomy Associations of America
PO Box 66
Fairview, TN 37062-0066
Phone: (800) 826-0826
E-mail: info@uoaa.org
Website: www.ostomy.org

This national, nonprofit organization offers support and information to people who have ostomies (procedures that surgically provide an artificial opening for elimination of wastes). It has an active discussion forum on its website where people can share experiences, advice, and problems.

Reach Out for Youth (ROFY) with Ileitis and Colitis
PO Box 857
Bellmore, NY 11710
Phone: (631) 293-3102
E-mail: info@reachoutforyouth.org
Website: www.reachoutforyouth.org

This volunteer organization provides support for young people with Crohn's and ulcerative colitis and their families in a variety of ways. In the Long Island, New York, area, it offers educational and social events for children and young people, help with dealing with medical issues, and the opportunity to talk about issues via Facebook, e-mail, or telephone.

For More Information

Books

Melissa Abramovitz. *Autoimmune Diseases*. Farmington Hills, MI: Lucent, 2011. This book describes and explores autoimmune diseases, why they occur, how they are diagnosed and treated, and how people live with these chronic diseases.

Peter Cartwright. *Coping Successfully with Ulcerative Colitis*. London: Sheldon, 2004. This book discusses the other major inflammatory bowel disease (IBD)—ulcerative colitis. Although written for adults, the book is easy to read and addresses people with the disease, their families, and friends. It discusses the causes, treatments, and diets for ulcerative colitis, as well as how to live a full, normal life.

Christina Potter. *Coping with Crohn's Disease and Ulcerative Colitis*. New York: Rosen, 2004. This book describes the symptoms of Crohn's and ulcerative colitis, how they are diagnosed, and how they are treated.

Penny B. Wolf. *I Still Dream Big: Stories of Living with Chronic Illness*. Bloomington, IN: AuthorHouse, 2009. The teens in this book have chronic diseases such as lupus, diabetes, and Crohn's disease. Their stories and experiences are chronicled as they face their diseases and learn to cope with their physical and emotional challenges with optimism and strength.

Websites

Crohn's Disease: PubMed Health (www.ncbi.nlm.nih.gov/pubmedhealth/PMH0001295). This page from the National Center for Biotechnology Information describes the signs and symptoms of Crohn's, along with diagnostic tests, treatments, and complications. Click the links to find out more about terms, tests, and symptoms, and mouse over the pictures to see enlarged images of conditions such as obstructions and abscesses.

David Garrard Speaks About Crohn's Disease (www.you
tube.com/watch?v=vujKfvTkF7s&feature=related). National
Football League (NFL) quarterback David Garrard gives a
speech about his successful fight against Crohn's disease at
Nemours Children's Clinic in Florida, posted on You Tube.

Growing Up IBD (www.growingupibd.org). Click the links to
read personal stories from young people with IBD and their
families.

**Slideshow: A Visible Guide to Inflammatory Bowel Disease
(IBD)** (www.webmd.com/ibd-crohns-disease/slideshow-in
flammatory-bowel-overview). With this set of images from
WebMD, visitors can see the normal gastrointestinal tract,
view the damage caused by Crohn's and ulcerative colitis,
and find pictures of complications and diagnostic tests.

Teens with Crohn's Disease Website (http://pages.prodigy
.net/mattgreen). This extensive website offers message
boards, chat rooms, help with diet and recipes, and a long
list of helpful links.

We Are Crohns.org (www.wearecrohns.org). This is a social net-
working site for people with Crohn's, ulcerative colitis, and
other IBDs. People share their stories, ask each other questions, and support one another. The site provides information about IBD, diet, and more. Visitors can also watch a
video about the group's efforts in San Francisco for World
Crohn's and Colitis Day in 2009.

Index

Picture Credits

About the Author

Toney Allman holds a bachelor of science degree from Ohio State University and a master's degree from the University of Hawaii. She currently lives in Virginia and has written more than thirty nonfiction books for students on a variety of medical and scientific topics.